War Against God's People

(The People of the Book)

Charlotte Wertheim

New Wine Press

New Wine Press
PO Box 17
Chichester
England PO20 6YB

Unless otherwise stated all Bible quotations are taken from the New King
James Version, copyright © 1983 by Thomas Nelson, Inc.

NIV – The Holy Bible, New International Version. Copyright © 1973,
1978, 1984 by International Bible Society. Used by permission.

AV – Authorised Verion of the Bible. Crown copyright.

AMP – Amplified Bible: Old Testament copyright © Zondervan
Publishing House; New Testament copyright © The Lockman
Foundation.

ISBN: 1 903725 13 5

Illustrations by Bernie Higgins and Mark Berry
Typeset by CRB Associates, Reepham, Norfolk
Printed in England by Clays Ltd, St Ives plc

Dedications

To the memory of my father H.J. Cross
who fought on his knees in prayer,
and in the trenches of World War I to defend
Britain against her enemies.

To my precious mother, Mary.
Her prayers saved my life.

To my two daughters, Nicola and Natasha
for their love and encouragement.

To Andy, my dear son-in-law,
whose knowledge of this subject both
challenged and inspired me.

To Jeffrey,
who always believed I should write.

To my Aunt Sadie (Sarah) Ferres,
for always believing in me.

To my friend, Martin Berger,
who helped co-ordinate this project.

To Ashley and Ruth Schmierer,
Senior Ministers, Christian Outreach Centre,
for 'seeing my heart'.

To David Harland, Senior Pastor,
Christian Outreach Centre,
for not allowing me to give up.

To my dear friend Ruth,
for always being there.

To June Cumper,
for her prayers.

Special thanks

To all my friends
without whose help this book could not have been written.

Liz Baxter, Bernie and Margaret Higgins,
Mark and Joanna Berry, Liz Mieli,
Simon Lewis – Assistant Pastor,
Christian Outreach Centre.

It really was a team effort.

Last but by no means least,
To the One whose name is above all names
The friend who stays closer than a brother.
Jesus, the Lover of my soul,
the Author and Finisher of my faith.

Contents

Preface

The midnight train was about to leave Victoria Station. Late arrivals, theatregoers, day trippers with bags full of shopping were running through the gates to board the last train heading for the coast. Among them were a group of young girls, excited, flushed and chattering wildly. The fact that they were wearing make-up, yet they were all dressed in school uniforms of red and grey, presented a strange sight in the late 1950s when girls in their early teens rarely wore make-up, especially greasepaint, the thick make-up used in the theatre, which looked strangely grotesque on their young faces.

Among the group were two girls who stayed closely together. Dark-haired, brown-eyed, they talked excitedly as an older woman, who was apparently their teacher, ushered them onto the train. One girl wore a golden Star of David around her neck, making her Jewishness obvious to all. The two girls looked like sisters.

It wasn't long before the train began to jerk into action and pick up speed. The group of girls, having been directed to their seats, settled down for the hour-long journey to the coast. Some read, others continued to chat with spasmodic bursts of laughter filling the air. One or two slept, it was after all late for girls of that age to be travelling, however, most of them were too excited to sleep.

Two of the girls got up and made their way down the corridor of the train in search of toilets.

The train was packed, some youths were standing in the corridor, the smell of beer and cigarette smoke pervaded the atmosphere, the laughter was loud and raucous. The two girls tried to push their way through the crowd of men, since no-one would make way for them.

Was it because of the alcohol which had obviously got the better of them, or the ludicrous sight of young girls wearing full stage make-up and school uniforms, or was it the Star of David shining brightly around a young girl's neck behind her open-neck shirt and loosely-tied school tie, that caused these youths to scream out obscenities about the Jews, swearing and cursing as they did?

I will never know the answer to these questions. What causes that anti-Semitic spirit to rise up? These thoughts have rolled around my head for many years, as I was one of those girls.

We were pupils from drama school and each had small parts in a Rogers and Hammerstein musical which had been running in the West End of London, hence the excitement and the stage make-up which we hadn't had time to remove without missing our train. Anyway when you are thirteen, to be seen out wearing make-up is an exciting experience in itself.

The rest of that night will remain in my mind for ever. First the shock, then the fear of the anger unleashed upon us. Why?

All I know is that something rose up inside me on that night that caused me to speak out against this attack, much to the surprise of my friend who asked me later why I had done this since I was a Gentile and the insults had been directed towards her, something all Jews were used to. I remember replying, *'I don't know, something got into my heart and I could not keep silent.'*

Now, after all these years, I know that the Holy Spirit was directing my life and planning my destiny even then.

The time of which I speak was about 1957, twelve years after World War II, the place London, England.

The same spirit that was behind the Third Reich still existed and was right here in our midst.

Of course I didn't understand these things then, but later on in my life when I began to study the history of Judaism and Christianity, I came to understand that there is a war going on and it is against the **people of the Book**, both Christian and Jew.

I also learned the spirit behind anti-Semitism is the spirit of anti-Christ; they are one and the same.

The following picture was taken off the Internet. I could not find any reference to its original source. It has been put there to convey a message, like all the pictures on the many **hate-sites** on the Web.

This is what compelled me to write this book.

Foreword

Some books are born of imagination and others are born by the inspiration of the Lord. I believe that Charlotte Wertheim's book, *War on God's People* was an inspired Divine appointment. While in the midst of writing 'The Nature of the Beast', an editorial piece for Vision for Israel's (an international humanitarian organization located in Israel) newsletter, a colleague called her on 11 September 2001 to tell her to turn on the news. It was during this moment that Charlotte unquestionably knew that the Lord had inspired her to address some of the issues of Islam and anti-Semitism. This was meant to be a part of a bigger picture and not simply an article.

I found Charlotte's book easy to read and very informative on these issues and their current impact on the world stage. It is a book that I would thoroughly recommend as required reading for the people of God, both Jews and Christians. It is a tool to broaden and to give a deeper understanding of the conflicts and the upheaval in the Middle East today. In my opinion, one of the greatest dangers facing the Church at this time is the lack of knowledge and the barrage of misinformation in such matters. This book goes a long way to help clear that up.

I have known Charlotte for over 10 years and both Batya and myself will always remember how she so willingly and warmly opened her house to us with our baby son during our first visit to England. She is a dear friend and serves as an active member on the board of Vision for Israel.

Barry Segal
Founder of Vision for Israel, International

Introduction

Wrath of ages

These words were the headlines in the *Sunday Times*, 15 October 2000, and this is indeed what is happening. There is a war against God's people, the people of the Book, both Jews and Christians.

This is a war, not just being waged by Osama Bin Laden and the likes of him and his followers, but by a false religious system that denies the gospel message of salvation through Jesus the Messiah; the deity of the Father, the Son and the Holy Spirit; the authority of the Word of God in both the Old and the New Testaments, and the existence of the nation of Israel.

Since the uprising of the Al Aqsa intifada, following Ariel Sharon's visit to the Al Aqsa Mosque on the Temple Mount on 28 September 2000, the suicide bombings and terrorist attacks have continued, so has the rise in Islamic extremism worldwide, culminating in the attack on the World Trade Centre in New York on 11 September 2001. All these events have forced both the world and the Church to focus on Israel.

Israel has always been a subject of debate that has caused people to become hot under the collar, both within Christian circles and outside of them. The very mention of the Jewish people or Israel as God's chosen race has caused people through-out the centuries and from all walks of life to break out in a hot sweat bordering on extreme fanaticism on one side or the other. The hatred or the love of these minority groups, who are pro or anti Israel, has caused the majority of Christians to ignore the subject altogether, perhaps hoping that if they don't think about these things, then maybe they will somehow disappear.

Not so. Israel and the Jewish people have been making the headlines in our daily newspapers for some time now. This tiny strip of land which was nothing more than a backwater from 70 AD to 1948 AD is once again a piece of real estate many believe is worth dying for.

My hope

The purpose of this book is not to educate but to inform. Not so much to teach but to inspire. The subject of Israel is not closed but open-ended, yet to be fulfilled. The books of Daniel and Revelation, along with the words of the prophets and the psalmists, are there for our careful consideration, waiting to be read.

Many brilliant authors and theologians have written on the subject, giving various interpretations of God's end-time plan for this world. Few have been able to ignore Israel and the Jewish people and the part they play in the final acts of world history, because Israel is centre stage and the spotlight is once again on Jerusalem, almost as if biblical history has had to come full circle in order for God's purposes to be fulfilled.

The hope of this author is to inspire the reader to see beyond the written word and to hear what the Holy Spirit is saying to the Church in this present age, not only through scriptures, though they be the source of all truth and the foundation upon which we build our theology, but also through world events as they appear to us through the media.

> 'The most beautiful thing we can experience is the mysterious. It is the source of all true art and all science. He to whom this emotion is a stranger, who can no longer pause to wonder and stand rapt in awe, is as good as dead, his eyes are closed.'   (Albert Einstein)

> *'For I do not desire, brethren, that you should be ignorant of this mystery lest you should be wise in your own opinion, that hardness in part has happened to Israel until the fullness of the Gentiles has come in. And so all Israel will be saved, as it is written:*
> *"The deliverer will come out of Zion,*
> *And He will turn away ungodliness from Jacob;*
> *For this is My covenant with them,*
> *When I take away their sins."*
> *Concerning the gospel they are enemies for your sake, but concerning the election they are beloved for the sake of the fathers.'*   (Romans 11:25–28)

Chapter 1

The History
Once Upon a Time

Hidden in the shifting whispering sands of the desert are the ruins of ancient civilisations whose rulers believed themselves to be gods. Great and glorious though their kingdoms were, they lived their day and are no more, lost in the mist of time.

Today, where is Babylon or the proud Medo-Persian Empire? Where is the Egypt of Cleopatra or the Greece of Alexander? Where are the Pharaohs and where are the Caesars? Once they were the objects of worship; now their deity is turned to dust, their immortality an illusion, encased forever in the bright sarcophagus of some museum.

Yet there is a nation older than them all, who was chosen not to be worshipped but to worship the one invisible God.

A nation who, despite rejection and persecution, was chosen to put no other god before Him, the Almighty. A people whose history is known worldwide from the world's oldest history book, who have been scrutinised as no other nation has. A people, not perfect but human, whose history is marked by their failure to meet the expectations of their God. A people whose history book records in detail, not their victories but the victories of **their God**. Not their successes but **His miracles** and **His mercy** upon them, who are described as a stubborn and stiff-necked people. A people, a nation and a book, so rooted in one tiny strip of land that neither distance – for they were scattered to the four corners of the earth – nor time, because for nearly two thousand years they wandered homeless – could separate them from the land of their origin and identity.

These people are the Jews, their nation is Israel, and their history book, the Bible, is the most published book in the world.

In 1948 the state of Israel was established. Today Israel, once again, is written on the map of world history, and the Jewish nation is the centre of world media attention.

Prophetic fulfilment

Historical events over the past century concerning the Jewish people and their return to the land of Israel have continued to prove the Bible to be word-perfect in its predictions. Jesus Himself predicted the destruction of Jerusalem in 70 AD and the scattering of the Jewish people all over the world (Luke 21:24; Jeremiah 9:16).

Under the Roman occupation of Jerusalem the Jewish people broke out in rebellion, warring against one another, divided into fanatical factions. Titus, the son of Emperor Vespasian, advanced upon Jerusalem leading an army of 100,000 troops. Titus gave strict orders to his troops not to destroy the temple ... but Jesus had prophesied its utter destruction:

> *'The days will come in which not one stone shall be left upon another that shall not be thrown down.'*   (Luke 21:6)

The historical records present a vivid picture of what happened:

> 'The direful day arrived, the destruction of the temple by the power of Rome. A soldier, then, upon the shoulders of a comrade succeeded in casting a torch through a door in the wall, which led to the chambers on the north side of the temple. Titus would have avoided this, for he was reluctant to destroy what was the glory of the whole world. The conflagration spread, however, fanned by a tempest; in the flames besieged and besiegers, locked in the final struggle, perished – their bodies against the very altar and the blood ran down the steps. The ground could not be seen for the dead. The furious priests brandished for weapons the leaden seats and spits of the temple service, and, rather than yield, threw themselves into the flames. Titus and his captains, entering the holy place, found it beautiful and rich beyond all report. The fire fastened upon all but the **imperishable rock**, and the Roman standards were set by the Eastern gate, and Titus received the salute of the legions as Emperor.'
> (*The Jews Ancient, Mediaeval and Modern*, Hosmer, p. 118)

Thus the prophecy of Jesus was fulfilled.

Today that rock remains on the Temple Mount under the golden Dome of the Rock. The rock where Abraham offered up

Isaac (but which the Muslims claim is the place where Abraham offered up Ishmael) is Islam's third most holy site. Thus, this tiny area of land has become the centre of dispute, involving Jews, Christians and Muslims in an age-old battle which could end in World War III.

The lies and propaganda continue but the Word of God does not lie and historical records support what our scriptures tell us.

Destruction of Jerusalem

The historian Josephus has recorded very detailed accounts of the destruction of the temple and the siege of Jerusalem. No less than 1,100,000 inhabitants were slain by the sword. Only 97,000 survived.

Many Jewish people had come from far and wide to celebrate the Jewish Feast of Passover only to be slain in Jerusalem. Forty years earlier at that same Feast, and on that same holy mount just outside the city of Jerusalem, Jesus had been crucified.

Now thousands of captives were impaled on crosses. The scriptures warn us:

'Whosoever falls on that stone will be broken.' (Luke 20:18)

Jesus's prophecy was literally fulfilled in the siege of Jerusalem:

'And they will fall by the edge of the sword, and be led away captive into all nations. And Jerusalem will be trampled by Gentiles until the times of the Gentiles are fulfilled.'

(Luke 21:24)

After Titus besieged Jerusalem 30,000 Jewish people were taken by him to Rome and used as slaves to build the Colosseum, with a seating capacity of 80,000. Christian martyrs were to provide sensational entertainment for Roman spectators in such theatres of death.

A people scattered

The final dispersion of the Jewish people was in AD 135, under the Emperor Hadrian. Simeon Ben Kozba defeated the Roman legions in AD 132 and became the head of an independent Jewish state. Rabbi Akiva, the great teacher/thinker of his day, renamed him Bar Kochba, or 'Star of the East', and believed him to be the Messiah referred to in the prophecy in Numbers 24:17, *'A Star shall come out of Jacob.'*

There was a two-year siege but the Jewish victory was short-lived. A fortress, south-west of Jerusalem, at Betar, was besieged and the remaining Jews were massacred on 9 Av 135, the anniversary of the destruction of the First and Second Temples.

The Bar Kochba revolt was the last armed rebellion in Judean history of the Holy Land and bears great significance to this current Israeli/Palestinian conflict, because it was at this time that the Latin word for 'Jewish' was banned by the Romans and the province was renamed 'Syria/Palaestina.' This name, which we now know as Palestine, has remained a subject of conflict to this day as it represents a negation of the Jewish right to the Holy Land. Emperor Hadrian also renamed Jerusalem 'Colonia Aelia Capitolina' and the city of Jerusalem was dedicated to the pagan god, Jupiter. On the site of the ruined Jewish Temple a new temple was erected to Jupiter, which has now been replaced by yet another temple, the Islamic Dome of the Rock, a travesty to God's holy dwelling place.

After this the Jews were a people without a country, scattered in many lands, resisting assimilation with the nations in which they sojourned, surviving in spite of cruel persecutions, despised, hated and destroyed in vast numbers. In spite of all the odds being stacked against this tiny race of people, the Jewish people have overcome their enemies – not by carnal weapons but the divine hand of God and by their simple racial pride and faith in their Creator. They have survived and increased by physical endurance and an indomitable will that has always believed in God's promises that one day He would bring them back to the land He gave to Abraham, Isaac and Jacob.

A people persecuted

The wandering Jew was hunted, tortured and put to death wherever he went: Russia, Poland, Germany, Spain, Holland, France, England. All hold records in their history books of the cruel persecution of the Jewish people.

Many countries banished them, including England in 1020 under the reign of King Canute. They were allowed to return at the time of the Norman conquest, followed by comparative peace until the Crusades.

During the reign of Richard the Lionheart in 1189–1199 (who led an army to the Holy Land to fight the Jews and Muslims and to take back the Holy Sepulchre) persecution broke out against the infidels in London. Not a Jewish household escaped without being robbed, tortured or murdered. Persecution spread to the provinces. York Castle witnessed the worst scene of all. The Chief Rabbi of York advised the Jews who had taken refuge in this fortress to yield up their lives to their Creator rather than be taken alive and further persecuted.

Husbands killed their wives and children and then themselves ... as the fires engulfed them. The last to remain alone was the Chief Rabbi who with one self-inflicted stroke joined his brothers in the flames. The next day the besiegers found only charred skeletons and a heap of ashes.

In 1263 in London, 400 Jews were massacred on Palm Sunday. In 1277 many Jews in Northampton were dragged to death by carthorses.

In 1278 in London, 680 Jews were imprisoned in the Tower, 290 were hanged.

In 1290 in London ... Expulsion ... All Jews to leave England for Feast of All Saints on 1 November.

This was the first general expulsion of Jews from any country in the mediaeval period (Roth, *History of the Jews in England*).

Edward I drove 16,500 Jews from England and for 400 years, until Cromwell granted permission for them to return, England was free of the Jewish people.

France drove 100,000 Jewish people out of their country in 1306 and the Crown confiscated their possessions. After ten years, however, they were recalled when the kingdom felt the need of their commercial abilities.

In Germany, at the time of the Black Death (1348–1350), Jewish people were accused of poisoning wells and springs. They were subjected to fearful tortures and innocent people were forced into confessions. One quarter of the population died of the plague and the Jewish people were blamed. In Strasbourg 2,000 victims were burned on a gigantic scaffold. Many were burned to death in Freibourg also. In Spires Jewish people were drowned. Whole communities throughout Germany were destroyed. Many Jewish people burned their own homes and perished in the flames rather than wait to die at the hands of those who hated them.

In Spain also the Jewish situation began to deteriorate with the Black Death in the middle of the fourteenth century. In 1391 there was an outbreak of pogroms in southern Spain which the authorities did little to control. Between 1411 and 1416 many

Jewish people converted to Christianity. These new Christians or *Conversos* were not popular and were never accepted on the grounds that their blood was contaminated. After 1492 Christians of a Jewish origin were regarded as a 'caste' different in essence from the pure 'Christian' population. These new laws concerning 'purity of blood' or *limpieza de sangre* reached a national level in 1547 at Toledo, the ecclesiastical capital. These rules were in evidence up until 1865 and had an immense influence on Spain, that remains to this day.

A people preserved

Wherever the Jewish people have gone they have faced persecution. How have they survived? By all natural laws the Jewish people should have been absorbed without trace by the various cultures and civilisations in which they have sojourned over the centuries.

So often you will hear Jewish people lament with words such as, 'We didn't ask to be chosen'. But chosen they are, for God's purposes, and He has marked them out among the nations. The Bible tells us:

> *'Their descendants shall be known among the Gentiles,*
> *And their offspring among the people.*
> *All who see them shall acknowledge them,*
> *That they are the posterity whom the LORD has blessed.'*
>
> (Isaiah 61:9)

Although the Jewish people were driven into ghettos and forbidden to own land, tortured, robbed and destroyed in vast numbers, their powers of endurance and their faith in the inexhaustible sufficiency of their God enabled them to survive, increase and gain positions of great eminence and power, often amassing great wealth.

> 'The Jew always begins with service and serviceableness, and ends with power and mastership. In the first stage he is difficult to grapple with. What are you to do with a man who simply stands and puts himself at your service? But in the second stage no one can get equal with him. We are all running to the Jews for help. And in a hundred years all will be with the Jews.'   (*Fallen Leaves* by Rosanof)

The Jewish people's uncanny ability to overcome and rise to the top surpassing the Gentiles in their achievements is their own undoing and is often the reason behind anti-Semitism.

> *'Surely the wrath of man shall praise You;*
> *With the remainder of wrath You shall gird Yourself.'*
>
> (Psalm 76:10)

Between 1881 and 1906 hundreds of thousands of Jewish people were killed in Russia, in organised massacres or pogroms. Hundreds of thousands fled to the USA. Over 1,000,000 Jewish people found asylum in America.

A people prospered

In America vast opportunities opened up to them. They became prominent financiers, lawyers, doctors, bankers and manufacturers. There was no stopping them.

Through their prosperity they were able to help their poor oppressed brothers in other lands. Vast sums of money were provided to enable these unfortunate Jewish people to emigrate to Palestine where they too began to prosper.

In 1936 the Iraq Petroleum Co. pumped 3,900,000 tons of crude oil through its pipeline from the Kirkuk oil fields in Iraq to Haifa, making this location one of the most important ports in the Mediterranean. Holland, France, Britain and America had interests in this enterprise together with five eastern nations.

The prosperity of the Jewish people, the oil and the rich minerals in the Dead Sea, gave Palestine an irresistible appeal to the covetousness of the surrounding nations, who knew full well that if they could control the Iraq/Mediterranean pipeline, they would have Europe eating out of their hands.

It's the same old story today as it was then. The world is ruled by the petrodollar and the governments that control the oil fields of the world will control the nations.

When America provided a safe haven for Jewish asylum seekers a century ago, she became an enemy to all those who hate Israel.

Chapter 2

A Land No-one Wanted

A desolate land

The Jewish people began to move back into Palestine in the late 1800s. The Turks, not the Arabs, controlled it at the time and it was a swamp-infested wasteland wanted by no-one including the Arabs. If the land of Israel had remained fertile and cultivated as it was before the Jews were scattered in 70 AD, then the conquering nations, the Romans, the Saracens, the Turks, the Egyptians, Caliphs, Latin Christians, the Mamelukes and the Ottoman Empire, to mention but a few, would have seized it for permanent occupation, but it did not appeal to them, barren as it was. How true the words of Jesus, '... *Jerusalem will be trampled by Gentiles* ... ' (Luke 21:24).

We can read in the diaries of famous travellers such as Sir Moses Montefiore, Rev. Robert Murray McCheyne, Mark Twain, and others, that one could ride from dawn until dusk, the length and breadth of the land, and see nothing but thorns and thistles as high as the horse's bridle. As far as the eye could see it was a scene of sorrowful desolation.

Jeremiah's prophesy was being fulfilled, in which he said:

> *'I will take up a weeping and a wailing for the mountains,*
> *And for the dwelling places of the wilderness, a lamentation,*
> *Because they are burned up,*
> *So that no one can pass through them;*
> *Nor can men hear the voice of the cattle.*
> *Both the birds of the heavens and the beasts have fled;*
> *They are gone.*
> *I will make Jerusalem a heap of ruins and a den of jackals.*
> *I will make the cities of Judah desolate, without an inhabitant.'*
>
> (Jeremiah 9:10–11)

For centuries the land, once flowing with milk and honey, was barren and sterile; its vineyards and olive groves perished. Having lapsed into a condition of utter poverty, the land was neglected and ignored even by its conquerors. No-one wanted this land!

Blessings and curses

Once again prophecies written thousands of years before were being fulfilled.

> ' "And it shall be that if you diligently obey My commandments which I command you today, to love the LORD your God and serve Him with all your heart and with all your soul, then I will give you the rain for your land in its season, the early rain and the latter rain, that you may gather in your grain, your new wine and your oil. And I will send grass in your fields for your livestock, that you may eat and be filled." Take heed to yourselves, lest your heart be deceived, and you turn aside and serve other gods and worship them, lest the LORD's anger be aroused against you, and He shut up the heavens so that there be no rain, and the land yield no produce, and you perish quickly from the good land which the LORD is giving you.'   (Deuteronomy 11:13–17)

By withholding the rain God's judgement upon the land of Israel made it undesirable to its conquerors and the surrounding nations, thus keeping it empty for its rightful inhabitants, the Jewish people.

In the last two centuries God has been bringing His people home to their land. The first Jewish colony was formed in Israel in 1870, when an agricultural school for boys was founded near Jaffa.

Many more were to follow. Hundreds of *kibbutzim* (colonies) brought thousands of settlers from Russia, Poland and Romania, the lands of the North, as prophesied in the book of Jeremiah:

> 'In those days the house of Judah shall walk with the house of Israel, and they shall come together out of the land of the north to the land that I have given as an inheritance to your fathers.'
> (Jeremiah 3:18)

The Jewish people purchased the land, which they proceeded to irrigate and farm. Many died of malaria in the process, but the dream of coming back to the Promised Land, and their Holy City of Jerusalem, had never left them. Upon their return the rains began to fall and the desert began to bloom, and Israel's restoration had begun. Between the years 1860 and 1862 the rainfall had increased by 60% and during this period the average rainfall in Israel was higher than in London and Berlin.

Life from the dead

We are on the edge of a war of apocalyptic proportions. With the threat of biological and nuclear weapons getting into the hands of fanatical terrorists with no regard for human life, anything could happen. We dare not make the same mistakes again, repeating the sins of our fathers against God's chosen people, the Jewish people and His land – the nation of Israel.

If and when the time should come when all that is left of animal and vegetable life is 'a valley of dry bones' and there is no-one left to speak of their existence, no-one who can remember the lives once lived, then who will tell their story?

Such was the scene revealed to Ezekiel, a Jewish priest and prophet sojourning in a strange land far from home. God said to him:

> 'Son of man, these bones are the whole house of Israel. They indeed say "Our bones are dry, our hope is lost, and we ourselves are cut off!" Therefore prophesy and say to them "Thus says the Lord GOD 'Behold, O My people, I will open your graves and cause you to come up from your graves and bring you into the land of Israel.''''
> (Ezekiel 37:11–12)

The Lord has kept His promise to return them to their land and the Jews, indestructible as they are, have survived to this day ... along with the nation of Israel. Its very existence demands our attention.

> 'For if their being cast away is the reconciling of the world, what will their acceptance be but life from the dead?'
> (Romans 11:15)

Chapter 3

Sudden Destruction

Times and epochs

The Bible is the inspired Word of God, revealed to the Jewish people, and handed down generation after generation, both orally and through the written word.

Without the Bible, Christianity becomes nothing more than folklore, legend or mythology. Our faith, *'the substance of things hoped for'* (Hebrews 11:1), if it is unsubstantiated by the Word of God, becomes a mere fantasy or illusion, much like any other religion with no sure foundation. But as the Word of God is our sure foundation, **the rock on which we stand**, then Israel and the Church together are God's physical and spiritual witnesses to a lost world that is heading for destruction.

For years Israel has been warning the US that the threat of Islamic terrorism is not against Israel alone – but it is against the whole of civilisation as we know it ... a danger to the entire world.

Softened by years of peace, and deluded into a false sense of security, America believed herself to be somehow untouchable.

When Israeli intelligence warned the US that Osama Bin Laden was planning an attack on America the reports went unheeded. Yet, as long ago as 1995, Benyamin Netanyahu, the former Israeli Prime Minister, wrote in his book *Fighting Terrorism*

> 'In the worst of such scenarios, the consequences could be not a car bomb but a nuclear bomb in the basement of the World Trade Centre.'

If we do not destroy terrorism, terrorism will destroy our civilisation.

Radical Islam is a global threat. As Prime Minister Ariel Sharon said in an Israeli national broadcast,

> 'The fight against terror is an international struggle of the free world against the forces of darkness who seek to destroy our liberty and our way of life. I believe that together we can defeat these forces of evil.'

These words echo the words of the Apostle Paul spoken so long ago when he warned the believers at Thessalonica,

> *'But concerning the times and the seasons, brethren, you have no need that I should write to you. For you yourselves know perfectly that the day of the Lord so comes as a thief in the night. For when they say, "Peace and safety!" then sudden destruction comes upon them, as labour pains upon a pregnant woman. And they shall not escape. But you, brethren, are not in darkness, so that this Day should overtake you as a thief. You are all sons of light and sons of the day. We are not of night nor of darkness. Therefore let us not sleep, as others do, but let us watch and be sober.'*
>
> (1 Thessalonians 5:1–6)

September 11
A corner was turned
In the human imagination
Now
Every conversation
Veers into
Apocalyptic speculation
Try
Averting your gaze
You cannot
The image
Persists
We all saw it
Death was
Live . . .
Before our eyes
Now
We can't ever close them
Again
Childhood
Has vanished

We stay awake in the dark
Eyes wide open
Waiting
For the next bombardment
Of Terror.   (C. Wertheim)

A wake-up call

On Tuesday 11 September just before 9 am in New York, as the business world was gearing itself up for another busy day, as European executives returned to their desks for the afternoon shift – the naked face of Islamic suicidal terrorism hit, with explosive force, the very heart of the American dream.

All that represented a modern capitalistic state, all that we deem to be free, civilised and democratic, is so obviously unguarded and penetrable.

The whole world watched in disbelief as the evil mind of the suicide bomber, brainwashed to welcome death, was exposed and magnified in big screen Hollywood style surrealism before our very eyes. Death was live before us on our TV screens.

The Pentagon and the World Trade Centre, the two symbols of military might and economic self-sufficiency in which the free world put their trust, crumbled into a heap of rubble beneath a cloud of dust.

11 September 2001 was a dark awakening for the civilised world.

But awaken we must, not only to the evil lurking in our midst, the fanaticism blind to its effect, terrible in its destruction, global in its reach, but to the still, small voice that comes *'not in the wind ... not in the earthquake, not in the fire,'* but in a whisper, deep into our heart and asks us, *Where do we stand and with whom?*

Perhaps this would be a good time to remind ourselves of the words printed on the American dollar bill (no less) 'In **God** we trust.'

When the cloud of dust that lingers over Washington and Manhattan has finally cleared, what will we see?

Will we see only the black holes, the remnants of the magnificent buildings that towered above us, symbolising all the glory, wealth and power of the modern age, the hopes and dreams of a brave new world?

Will we remember forever with fear and trembling the moment of impact as two opposing forces collided and exploded before us, one representing a system that provided for all our creature comforts and (dare I say) many of us believed would endure forever, or at least for our lifetime, the other a force so dark, so menacing and so intense that nothing, not even death, can destroy it?

> *'For we do not wrestle against flesh and blood, but against principalities, against powers, against the rulers of the darkness of this age, against spiritual hosts of wickedness in the heavenly places.'*   (Ephesians 6:12)

High above the Manhattan skyline we will never forget the terrible images of bodies falling, lives destroyed in an instant, flesh and blood mingled with the rubble of high technology, lives invested in a system that could so easily be reduced to dust like all the systems or civilisations that have gone before us, lost forever under a cloud of smoke. How could this be?

On 11 September 2001 in the skies over America two dreams collided, two ideologies, one of an earthly paradise based on economic growth and the superiority of business over political and spiritual power, the other a paradise into which only martyrs can enter through the flames of Islamic Holy War.

Is it a dream or reality that we believe? Ideology or Theology? God or Mammon? Is it Might or Power or the **Spirit of the Living God** in whom we put our trust?

> *' "Not by might, nor by power, but by My Spirit,"*
> *Says the LORD of hosts.'*   (Zechariah 4:6)

Now that the dust has cleared and the bereaved and broken-hearted return to their desks at the Pentagon and in Manhattan, and somewhere another suicide bomber waits for a call to action, what do we see? Can we lift up our eyes to the hills and see beyond the chaos? What is the **One who sits upon the throne, who created the heavens and the earth**, trying to tell us?

A burdensome stone

Was it coincidental that only a week before this terrorist attack on New York and Washington, America had walked out of the Durban Conference on Racism, along with Israel and the tiny nation of Micronesia? This event let the whole world know where they stood concerning Israel.

Although the attack on America had been prepared months or even years before, the timing cannot be ignored. In the end those who come against Israel will reap their own destruction, for it says in Scripture:

> *'For thus says the LORD of hosts: "He sent Me after glory, to the nations which plunder you; for he who touches you touches the apple of His eye.'* (Zechariah 2:8)

The destiny of Jerusalem determines the destiny of the whole world:

> *'...I will make Jerusalem a cup of drunkenness to all the surrounding peoples ... And it shall happen in that day that I will make Jerusalem a very heavy stone for all peoples; all who would heave it away will surely be cut in pieces, though all nations of the earth are gathered against it.'* (Zechariah 12:2–3)

The ultimate goal of Israel's enemies is her demise. The nature of the beast is trans-national globalisation, in other words his plan is to take on the whole world. Whether it be in the name of Mohammed or Hitler, Islam or Neo-Nazism, Anti-Semitism is the spirit of Antichrist and Jesus warned us saying in Matthew 24:5,

> *'For many will come in My name saying, "I am the Christ," and will deceive many.'*

Chapter 4

Tidal Waves of Hatred

Rewriting history

The prince of the power of the air (Ephesians 2:2), manipulating the use of the media, has been rising up with lies and propaganda against Israel, consistently deconstructing Jewish history from Solomon's Temple to Auschwitz.

Journalists and news commentators ignorant of the Word of God are spreading a new version of history over the global network worldwide.

The unbelieving world and liberal Christianity that has little or no knowledge of the Bible is being sucked into this web of deceit by the media's distortions.

> 'O, what a tangled web we weave when first we practise to deceive.'　　　　　　　　　　　　　　　　　(Sir Walter Scott)

The Jewish people are being demonised on radio and television in the Islamic world. The news media is state-controlled but even in the theatre and arts, film-makers, song writers, authors and cartoonists are depicting the Jew in a grotesque, sub-human form, a pollution to all mankind like a virus that is poisoning the world. The words and the propaganda of Nazi Germany echo in our ears.

Just as in the Third Reich so it is in the Islamic world – men, women and children are being brainwashed. They are being taught a revised version of history in which a chosen people, the one true God and state of Israel are non-existent.

The Bible – the Word of God, is being systematically manipulated, re-written and struck off the records of human history in the Moslem world.

Cover of a popular French edition of *Protocols*

c. 1934

Covers of *Protocols*

'...Probably the most widely distributed
book in the world after the Bible...'
(Norman Cohn)

Top row (left to right): French, German
Bottom row (left to right): English, Russian

Covers of *Protocols*

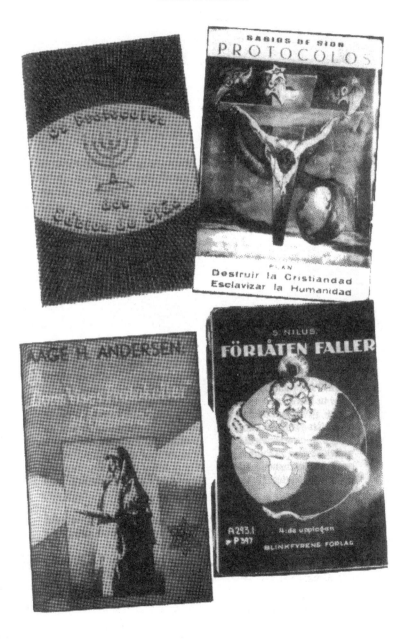

Top row (left to right): Portuguese, Spanish
Bottom row (left to right): Danish, Swedish

Cover of a Brazilian edition of *Protocols*

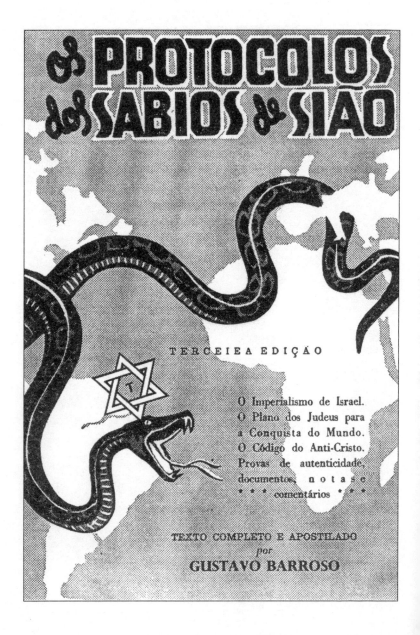

São Paulo, 1937

Cover of a popular French edition of *Protocols*

c. 1934

The Syrian Minister of Defence Mustafa Tlas published a book on the Blood Libel and a revised edition of Mein Kampf in 1983. It became a best seller in the Arab-speaking world. Today in 2001 his book on the Blood Libel (a myth accusing Jews of drinking Gentile blood) is being made into a film. A Palestinian script writer is being used and the author, Mustafa Tlas, is said to be donating 5% of the profits to the Palestinian Intifada.

The Blood Libel of Damascus 1840 together with *The Protocols of the Elders of Zion* and other anti-Semitic literature was used by Hitler as the ideology behind the Third Reich. *The Protocols* are second only in publication to the Bible and have rightly been called the Bible of anti-Semitism. They are a forgery written in the nineteenth century. Widely published after World War I, they were used to justify the massacre of the Jews in the Russian Civil War, and were exploited by Goebbels, Hitler's Minister of Propaganda, in 1942. Today this Anti-Semitic propaganda continues to be distributed throughout the world, especially in the Arab nations on their web-sites, radio stations and news-papers. However, because of the power of the media and modern technology these Anti-Semitic images are available to us all on hate-sites worldwide.

The nature of the beast is death

Brainwashed to welcome death, the mind-set of the suicide terrorists who attacked New York and Washington is the same as the suicide bombers who blew themselves and their victims to smithereens in the busy streets of Jerusalem, the discotheque in Tel Aviv, and outside a school filled with Jewish children in Israel, to mention only a few of the acts of terror perpetrated against the Jewish nation, victimising and killing dozens of innocent men, women and children.

Young men trained in terrorism from childhood, religiously devout and filled with a chilling dedication and hatred for the enemies of Islam, wait for their moment of martyrdom to come. This is what they live for, to die for Allah.

Just as Hitler's passionate oratory roused the Hitler Youth to total and absolute dedication, national and religious fanaticism, just as the SS or Aryan 'pure bloods' were given charge over the Nazi prize relic, the 'blood flag' drenched in the blood of the martyrs from the Munich Putsch, so the nature of the beast has not changed and tomorrow's suicide bomber will have received his call to martyrdom as young as ten, in a Mosque while at prayer.

> 'I will take my soul in my hand
>   and toss it into the Abyss of death.'
>   (This is a poem from Palestinian school books;
>   5th, 6th and 12th grades.)

As Hitler stirred up the masses into a fervour, so the teachers in the schools and the holy men or imam in the mosque can in one single, chilling moment switch the mind of many of their devoted followers into martyr mode. Young men are chosen to die for Allah.

Hatred of the Jews

> 'The hatred of the Jewish people has been and remains a blot on the soul of mankind. The Anti-Semite rejoices at any opportunity to vent his malice. The times have made it unpopular, in the West, to proclaim openly a hatred of Jews. This being the case the Anti-Semite must constantly seek new forms and forums for his poison. How he must revel in the new masquerade. He does not hate Jews, he is just Anti-Zionist! When people criticise Zionism they mean Jews, this is God's own truth.'
> (A selection from the writings of Martin Luther King Jnr.)

According to the philosopher Voltaire, the crime of the Jewish people was none other than being born.

The nature of the beast does not change. The enemy always condemns, always blames, always points the finger of suspicion at the very ones who are the victims of his atrocities. Was not even Jesus accused of being Beelzebub, the Prince of Demons?

The devil has only one plan, from the temptation of Adam and Eve in the Garden, to the temptation of Christ in the wilderness, even to this present day. His aim has always been to make God out to be a liar.

It should not be surprising that the Jewish people and Israel, and the Hebrew Scriptures (the Bible) which contain the title deeds of the land of Israel, should be under such vicious attack.

> *'The* LORD *made a covenant with Abram, saying: "To your descendants I have given this land, from the river of Egypt to the great river, the River Euphrates."'*   (Genesis 15:18)

The land promised to Abraham goes beyond the boundaries of modern-day Israel and includes the disputed territories. This promise was unconditional.

> *'Sarah your wife shall bear you a son, and you shall call his name Isaac; I will establish My covenant with him for an **everlasting** covenant, and with his descendants after him.'*
>
>   (Genesis 17:19, my emphasis)

Although Abraham had eight sons in all, the covenant was established with Isaac (Genesis 16:15; 25:1–2).

Standing with Israel

The devil knows his time is running out. Messiah is coming again. The trumpet is being blown in Zion to arouse the nations so that God's people, the true Church and believing Israel, his two witnesses, will stand together as one glorious new man.

Many Islamic states that succeeded in turning an Anti-Racism Conference in Durban into the most racist meeting since World War II had hundreds of years of anti-Jewish propaganda on which to build their attack. They chose an ideal arena, with the whole world witnessing the lies and accusations made against Israel by the fifty-five Moslem Bloc Nations.

The nature of the beast has not changed. If he had known the power of the resurrection, he never would have crucified Jesus. It is this very nature of the beast that brings its own downfall. Ultimately God will have His way and it will be the beast which will be crushed for ever. We should not be surprised when President George W. Bush walked out of the Durban conference, along with Israel and Micronesia, the tiniest nation. God uses the small, the weak and the insignificant to shame the proud and the mighty and those who would be wise in their own estimation.

> *'For, it is written:*
>   *"I will destroy the wisdom of the wise,*
>   *And bring to nothing the understanding of the prudent."*
> *Where is the wise? Where is the scribe? Where is the disputer of this age? Has not God made foolish the wisdom of this world?'*
>   (1 Corinthinas 1:19–20; see also Isaiah 29:14)

Perhaps this is a wake-up call to each and every one of us to listen to the still, small voice in our heart, because it's heart to heart that God always reveals Himself.

Perhaps we should ask ourselves, as President Bush had to ask himself, at the Durban Conference: Where do I stand? What am I to do? Whose side am I on?

Israel is the only democracy in the Middle East. She sticks out like a sore thumb in the Arab world. Tyrannical nations need an external enemy to blame for the woes of their own oppressed people.

Just as Hitler needed the Jewish people as scapegoats for his own evil plans and purposes for world domination, so all tyrants need an enemy to blame.

The nature of the beast has not changed and this campaign of hatred will continue as long as he is loosed in the earth:

> *'and he cast him into the bottomless pit, and shut him up, and set a seal on him, so that he should deceive the nations no more . . . '*
> (Revelation 20:3)

Who owns these last remains?

Dawn . . . will come . . .
And what will we have learned?
The fires continue to burn
The earth is strewn with human flesh
Our brother's blood is calling out to us from the ground
Our brother . . .

Who is our brother?
Where is our brother?
Our mother, our sister?
Who's who among the dead?
This tangled mass of DNA?
Was this someone's father?
Was this someone's child?
Who owns these last remains?

Now . . . we want answers
That our governments could never give us
Now . . . we want solutions
That our weapons could not provide
Now . . . our rotting flesh cries out
To the One who created all flesh . . .
If . . . there is a God . . . who owns these last remains?

If ... there is a God
Let Him identify each fingerprint
If ... there is a God
Let Him decipher the genetic code
Determining our kith and kin
If there is a God ... let Him tell us Who?
Who is our brother?
And ... If there is a God
Can we bear to hear
What He will say?   (C. Wertheim)

'Am I my brother's keeper?'   (Genesis 4:9)

Chapter 5

My Appointed Times
A Vision in Babylon

The day of reckoning

In Leviticus 23 God calls the Feasts or Jewish Holy Days of Israel *'My appointed times.'*

The Jewish New Year 5762 began seven days after the terrorist attacks on New York and Washington.

Rosh Hashanah begins in the seventh month of the Jewish calendar and is the civil New Year. The first month or religious New Year is at the time of Passover.

Rosh Hashanah is a solemn time of self-searching and penitence leading up to Yom Kippur or the Day of Atonement. The rabbis tell us that on the New Year all the inhabitants of the world pass before Him (the Almighty) like flocks of sheep. As it is said,

> 'He who fashioned the hearts of them all understands all their doings.'   (Rosh Hashanah 1:2 Rabbinical Teachings)

On Yom Kippur 2001, Jewish people flocked to the synagogues, the events of 11 September heavy on their hearts. Many wear plimsolls on this day in order to tread more softly upon the earth ... there was a silence, a solemnity about this year. Some of the congregants had volunteered to stand guard outside the local synagogue and were chatting with the two policemen on guard. Strangers were asked to identify themselves on entering. Despite the holiness of Yom Kippur these things were necessary. Was this year different to any other year for Jews?

Outside synagogues up and down the nation this procedure is not new, security is a regular concern, and the guards are there at every meeting and have been for a long time, not only to protect the Jewish people from the Nazi skinheads with knives, but also because of the Islamic Fundamentalists and radical Arab Nationalists who hate Israel and hate Jews. We remember only too well just over a year ago when a Jewish theology student was stabbed more than twenty times in a frenzied attack while he was reading the Psalms on a bus in North London.

Confronting a common enemy

'Stabbed for Being Jewish' were the headlines in the *Evening Standard*, 17 October 2000.

Later that month orthodox Jews in Golders Green were afraid to wear a *kipah* (skull cap) as leaflets had been distributed by extreme factions in the Muslim community calling for the killing of Jews (*Jewish Chronicle*, 27 October 2000). A young boy of 15 said he was afraid because of the threats against Jewish people in Britain.

When the planes crashed into the twin towers the Jews wept, mourned and were angered along with the rest of the world at the appalling horror of the attack.

When President Bush and Prime Minister Blair declared war, the Jewish people breathed a sigh of relief, now they were not alone in their fight against terrorism. Now the rest of the democratic world was going to participate in a war against terrorism that the Jews had been fighting for decades.

The suicide bombers in Tel Aviv and New York are essentially the same to most British Jews. Whether the methods of destruction are planes controlled by terrorist groups, or bombs strapped to a martyr's own body as he stalks his victims, in a discothque, a busy shopping mall or a crowded bus, the mind of the suicide bomber is the same, crude, unjustifiable and murderous – **and these terrorists threaten our very existence**.

Media twists

Yet, what we read in the newspapers and watch on TV reveals a different story. It seems the media sees Israel as the aggressor and the Palestinians as the victims. Somehow or other it seems the Jewish people are always to be blamed **just for being Jewish**. The tide turned against Israel the moment she stopped being alone in her fight against Islamic terrorism. Now she shares her fate with the rest of the world, we are all victims ... Jerusalem, and the Al Aqsa Intifada, is the spark that set the whole world on fire.

America, who has helped Israel from a safe distance, but never really wanted to get their hands dirty, has now been dragged into the whole sorry mess, when terrorism hurled itself at the World Trade Centre and unleashed all its fury reserved for any **friend of Israel**.

Who can afford to bear this burden? Like Pontius Pilate the world wants to wash its hands of the whole affair. Overnight Israel has become a lethal liability, and anyone who touches her will get their hands burned. No one can afford to take the risk.

'I will make Jerusalem an immovable rock for all the nations. All who try to move it will injure themselves.' (Zechariah 12:3 NIV)

Voice of the prophet

The only mention of the Hebrew phrase Rosh Hashanah (this solemn time of repentance, leading up to Yom Kippur or Day of Atonement) is found in Ezekiel 40 and was recorded by the prophet during his exile in Babylon.

Ezekiel saw both in person and in vision the ultimate end of Jerusalem. In fact the whole of the first part of the book records this. He was taken into captivity at the age of twenty-five and was in the first deportation to Babylon.

His story is interesting because he was both a prophet and a priest, the son of Zadok the high priest. Had he remained in Jerusalem he would have begun his priestly duties at the age of thirty, just like Jesus, but instead he was called by God to be a prophet at this age, while in captivity many miles from the Holy City. He lived in Kifi in Baghdad and died there. He was never to return to Jerusalem and his tomb is there to this day.

'In the twenty-fifth year of our captivity, at the beginning of the year, on the tenth day of the month, in the fourteenth year after the city was captured, on the very same day the hand of the LORD was upon me; and He took me there. In the visions of God He took me into the land of Israel and set me on a very high mountain; on it toward the south was something like the structure of a city.'
(Ezekiel 40:1–2)

'Also the tenth day of this seventh month shall be the Day of Atonement. It shall be a holy convocation for you; you shall afflict your souls, and offer an offering made by fire to the LORD.'
(Leviticus 23:27)

A vision in Babylon

It was in present-day Iraq that Ezekiel received the vision. He was transported in the Spirit to the new city of Jerusalem and he saw the New Temple standing on the site which is now occupied by the Dome of the Rock and the Al Aqsa Mosque. This area called the Temple Mount, has become the central symbol of the Palestinian 'Al Aqsa Intifada' and the intensification of the present conflict regarding the future of Jerusalem. The site is jointly administered by Jews and Muslims who both want total control. Moreover we frequently hear of Muslims who declare their readiness to sacrifice their lives '**in defence of the mosques.**'

On this Day of Atonement, so long ago, probably while he was at prayer, in a foreign land far from his beloved Jerusalem, Ezekiel is given a supernatural glimpse of the future temple that will one day stand in the Holy City.

Ezekiel goes on to record the precise details of the temple as revealed to him by God.

> *'And behold, the glory of the God of Israel came from the way of the east. His voice was like the sound of many waters; and the earth shone with His glory.'*   (Ezekiel 43:2)

> *'He said to me, "Son of man, this is the place of My throne and the place of the soles of My feet, where I will dwell in the midst of the children of Israel forever ... '*   (Ezekiel 43:7)

> *'Son of man, describe the temple to the house of Israel, that they may be ashamed of their iniquities; and let them measure the pattern. And if they are ashamed of all that they have done, make known to them the design of the temple and its arrangement, its exits and its entrances, its entire design and all its ordinances, all its forms and all its laws. Write it down in their sight, so that they may keep its whole design and all its ordinances, and perform them.'*   (Ezekiel 43:10–11)

> *'For the LORD has chosen Zion;*
> *He has desired it for His habitation:*
> *This is My resting place forever;*
> *Here I will dwell, for I have desired it.'*

>   (Psalm 132:13–14)

Zion is another name for Jerusalem. This is the most sacred spot in the eyes of God and in the future the millennial temple will be located here. The will and the aspiration to build the Temple still beats in the heart of the nation of Israel.

> *'And they shall rebuild the old ruins,*
> *They will raise up the former desolations,*
> *And they shall repair the ruined cities,*
> *The desolations of many generations.'*   (Isaiah 61:4)

Ezekiel's vision was describing the restoration of the Land of Israel, a supernatural location filled with the glory of God.

Headlines in *The Guardian* 14 February 2002 '**US Targets Saddam – Pentagon and CIA making plans for war against Iraq this year.'**

Who but God Himself could have planned it? In what is now present-day Iraq, where Saddam Hussein plots his own evil schemes against Israel and the West, God had already laid down His own end-time plan for Jerusalem and for His future reign here on earth. This is God's promise: **He will come and dwell in Jerusalem, His Kingdom will be on earth, as it is in heaven.**

> *'...and the name of the city from that day shall be:*
> THE LORD IS THERE.'   (Ezekiel 48:35)

Ezekiel's vision is very similar to that of the Apostle John:

> *'Then I, John, saw the holy city, New Jerusalem, coming down out of heaven from God, prepared as a bride adorned for her husband. And I heard a loud voice from heaven saying, "Behold the tabernacle of God is with men, and He will dwell with them, and they shall be His people, and God Himself will be with them and be their God.'*   (Revelation 21:2–3)

Chapter 6

Who Are the Palestinians?

What's in a name?

The present day Palestinian/Israeli conflict needs to be addressed historically. First of all where did the name Palestine come from? Who are the Palestinians?

Palestine was never an Arab nation, because the name was given by the Romans as a derogatory term, not to a people group, but to a region of Judea. It came from the ancient Philistines who were wiped out in 1200 BC and have no connection with the present-day Arabs.

Just as Essex is an area in the UK, but has no government or prime minister, so Palestine is a region, not a nation.

Before 1948 and the rebirth of the State of Israel, both Arabs and Jews who lived in this region were considered Palestinians. The Jewish newspaper was called *The Palestine Post*, now called *The Jerusalem Post*. The Jews would hardly have named their own newspaper after another people group.

There has never been a land known as Palestine governed by a people called Palestinians. There is, in fact, no such thing as a **Palestinian culture** as distinct from other Arab cultures.

Jordan, a nation created by Great Britain in 1922, was in control of the region of Palestine when Israel captured Jerusalem in 1967. It was never taken from **Palestinians**.

Yasser Arafat himself fondly recalls a childhood in Jerusalem, describing his place of birth as a stone house next to the Western Wall where he lived with his Uncle Saud. However in 1997 the book *Les sept vies de Yasser Arafat* written by two French biographers Christophe Boltanski and Ichan El Tahri quote: 'Mr Palestine was born on the shores of the Nile.'

The researchers discovered that Arafat was born on 4 August 1929 in Cairo. He lived in Cairo until he was 28 and identified himself as an Egyptian, travelling to Russia in 1968 on an Egyptian passport. His claim to be of Palestinian origin, a victim of Zionism who lost everything when Israel came into existence, is all part of the Palestinian myth.

Palestinians are Arabs, indistinguishable from Syrians, Iraqis, Lebanese, Jordanians etc. who control 99.9% of the Middle East lands. Israel represents 1/10 of 1% of the landmass.

Birthed into war

The establishment of the state of Israel in May 1948 provoked such rage in the Arab nations that five of them promptly attacked her, violating UN resolutions, with the intention of destroying Israel completely. The Arab nations advised those Arabs, then living and working in Israel, to abandon their homes. They were promised not only to return and occupy their homes once again, once the battle had been won, but also that they would gain possession of Jewish houses, so sure were the Arabs of victory. However, things did not go according to plan. 600,000 became homeless refugees. The Arab nations, who could so easily have absorbed them, refused to do so, using their plight as a political weapon against Israel.

Khaled El–Azm, a former prime minister of Syria, writes in his memoirs:

> 'Since 1948, it is we who demanded the return of the refugees to their country, while it is we who made them leave it. Is this a wise and established policy? Is this the coordination in planning? We brought disaster upon one million Arab refugees by inviting them to leave their land, their homes, their work and their industry. We have rendered them dispossessed, unemployed, whilst every one of them had work or a trade by which he could gain his livelihood. We exploited them in executing crimes of murder, arson and throwing bombs upon houses and vehicles carrying men, women and children. All this in the service of political purposes in Lebanon and Jordan.'

Here is written proof that the Palestinian refugees, and the human suffering inflicted upon them, is the responsibility of the Arab nations. It cost the UN over two billion dollars and placed an enormous burden on the Israeli economy.

The immense media coverage of the Palestinian refugee problem completely outweighs any references to the 800,000 Jews who were forced to leave their Arab homelands in 1948, leaving behind vast amounts of property and possessions which were taken by the Arabs.

Between 1948 and 1951 Israel absorbed Jewish refugees from Tunisia, Morocco, Libya, Algeria, Aden, Syria, Lebanon and Egypt, who represented almost the total population of Israel in 1948. With limited resources Israel did her best to accommodate these Jewish refugees, unlike her Arab neighbours, who refused to give shelter to their own people whom **they** had made homeless.

The world media paid no attention to the Jewish refugees, nor has the UN ever mentioned them. Because Israel took responsibility for her own people, she has nothing to hide, unlike the Arab world, who would choose to spread lies and propaganda against Israel, rather than allow the truth to be known.

Who owns Jerusalem?

In the years between 1948/1967 when East Jerusalem and the West Bank were controlled by Jordan, there were no demands being made in the Arab world for an independent Palestinian state with Jerusalem as its capital.

It is interesting to note that it is only since 1967 and the Six Day War over Jerusalem (the time when Jerusalem came back into Jewish hands after nearly 2000 years of bitter battles and much bloodshed between Jews, Arabs and Christians) that moves have been made to settle Palestinians on the West Bank and East Jerusalem and even more blood has been shed. Only since Jerusalem once again became the Jewish capital of Israel did the Arab world begin to shout about displaced Palestinians. The battle is and always was over the City of Jerusalem.

The Palestinians are the pawns being used in a political and religious chess game, in which the contesting players are Allah and the God of Abraham, Isaac and Jacob, the God of Israel. We know who will win, and then the world will see who is the Almighty, the creator of heaven and earth, the God above all gods.

The Bible is a futuristic book of which a quarter of all the verses contain predictions about the future. It is also a very accurate book. Over 80% of the predictions have already become historical facts. Since the remaining 20% are all concerned with the end of history, which obviously has not happened yet, the Bible has achieved 100 % accuracy.

All the biblical predictions are concerned with the nation of Israel and the Jewish people. God has a plan and the Bible tells us what the future will be for planet earth. The destiny of Jerusalem determines the destiny of the world.

Whose report shall we believe? Whose plan will come to fulfilment? Is there any connection between what we are reading in our newspapers and the biblical prophecies?

What's news?

There have been numerous ceasefires between Arafat and Israel none of which ever really got off the ground. It was just a matter of time before the killings started again. The founder of Hamas, the militant network behind the repeated suicide bomb attacks against Israeli civilians, Sheikh Ahmed Yassin said, 'The US wants to open a battle against Islam. They should know that religious battles are long and wild. In the end they will be defeated.' The Syrian-based Palestinian National Liberation Movement also pledged to wreck the ceasefire. A spokesman said, 'We will continue our legitimate and just struggle side-by-side with all the Palestinian and Islamic national factions until we expel the Israeli occupation and liberate Palestine.'

Chapter 7

No Compromise

A people of destiny

Israel will never compromise when its very existence is at stake. The country has been in a state of war that started five hours after it came into being in 1948. So what's new? There have been armed truces, but this ongoing state of war has never ceased in 52 years.

The two-state solution proposed by the UN in November 1947 was rejected by the Arabs and the fact of their non-acceptance remains unchanged. The Israelis were willing to accept a Palestinian state. The Palestinians, however, have never truly accepted a Jewish state, and even though many left-wing Jews, exhausted by continual war, do still dream of a multi-cultural Israel with Arabs and Jews living together in peace, the truth is becoming more obvious day by day, that within an Islamic state there would be no room for practising Jews.

Afghanistan is an extreme example of what can happen to non-Muslims living in a Muslim state. On 23 May 2001 it was decreed by the authorities in Kabul that all Hindus be required to wear a strip of yellow cloth sewn onto their shirt pockets. Haven't we heard this somewhere before?

The same forces that turned Germany into Nazi Germany still exist in the world. Israel is accused in the media and through anti-Israel propaganda to be all things evil and was described in a two-part article by General Hassan Sweilem in the Egyptian government- sponsored weekly *October* magazine as 'full of bad qualities, base and loathsome.' The series included anti-Semitic remarks attributed to George Washington and Benjamin Franklin, first used in a vicious forgery that appeared in 1935 in Germany in the Nazis Handbook *The Jewish Question* (*Daily Telegraph*,

10 February 2001). Meanwhile, the truth is that Arab Israelis have more freedom than their brothers anywhere in the Arab world.

> 'Recently a 48-year old Arab Israeli left his two wives and 10 children, strapped explosives to his body, said his prayers and then blew himself up at an Israeli railway station, killing three innocent people and injuring scores of others. It was a terrible thing to do, but the Israeli government is paying his wives roughly £1,600 a month and providing them with two houses so that they and the children are properly provided for. However heinous this act of terrorism, he was an Israeli citizen and so his widow and children are entitled to the full benefits the law provides.'
>
> (*The Mail on Sunday*, 23 September 2001)

The Jewish people have survived for more than 2000 years on their unshakeable faith in God's promises that one day they would return to their Promised Land. At every Passover in lands far away from Israel they would lift their glasses and drink a toast, 'Next Year in Jerusalem'. Even in the death camps of Nazi Germany this prayer saw them through to another day, and that single prayer is heard and remembered by every Jew almost as soon as they can speak. Nothing on earth will ever separate the Jews from their Holy Land again ... nothing on earth.

Sound of war

God's appointed time for the vision revealed to Ezekiel was recorded carefully in Chapter 40:1. It was the Day of Atonement, the only day in the year when the high priest would go in behind the veil and enter the Holy of Holies in the Temple at Jerusalem.

Just as in the vision of Ezekiel when he saw the Creator in all His glory seated upon a crystal throne above the intersected wheels surrounded by eyes, so the Almighty is omnipresent and all seeing, and He who watches over Jerusalem never slumbers nor sleeps.

Rosh Hashanah is also called the Feast of Trumpets when the shofar is blown in the synagogues.

> '*Then the* Lord *spoke to Moses, saying, "Speak to the children of Israel saying 'In the seventh month, on the first day of the month, you shall have a sabbath rest, a memorial of blowing of trumpets, a holy convocation.'"'* (Leviticus 23:23–24)

'And the LORD *spoke to Moses, saying: "Make two silver trumpets for yourself; you shall make them of hammered work; you shall use them for calling the assembly and for directing the movement of the camps ... When you go to war in your land against the enemy who oppresses you, then you shall sound an alarm with the trumpets, and you will be remembered before the* LORD *your God, and you will be saved from your enemies." '*

(Numbers 10:1–2, 9)

The trumpets were to be blown at appointed feasts; they were to lead the congregation to worship and to battle.

'For the trumpet will sound, and the dead will be raised incorruptible, and we shall be changed.'   (1 Corinthians 15:52)

'For the Lord Himself will descend from heaven with a shout, with the voice of an archangel, and with the trumpet of God. And the dead in Christ will rise first.'   (1 Thessalonians 4:16)

If, as the newspapers are warning us, we are on the brink of war, then God certainly has not left us unprepared.

Chapter 8

Rewriting History

New face of anti-Semitism

History has a habit of repeating itself. As Solomon said, *'There is nothing new under the sun'* (Ecclesiastes 1:9). There is a spiritual battle being waged in the heavenlies over Jerusalem and the sovereignty of Israel and the Jewish people over the Temple Mount, the area on which Solomon's temple and the temple built by Herod once stood, the area purchased by David from Araunah the Jebusite (2 Samuel 24:18–25), which was paid for lock, stock and barrel. The Bible contains the receipt and title deeds for the land of Israel.

The devil has targeted the Jewish people for destruction since time immemorial in an attempt to nullify God's covenant and to discredit His Word.

Arafat repeatedly declares that there never was a temple built by Solomon nor was there a second Temple built by Herod, the temple in which Jesus taught and over which He prophesied, saying that it would be destroyed – *'not one stone shall be left here upon another'* (Matthew 24:2) – and so it was in 70 AD, for it was destroyed by the Romans who separated each stone to remove the gold that had melted in the fire and run down in between the stones.

This ancient site of the Temple Mount has now been re-named Haram al Sharif by the Muslims, and Israel's supreme Muslim cleric, the Mufti of Jerusalem, issued a Fatwa (a religious decree) on 20 February 2001 that the whole of the Temple Mount area, including the Wailing Wall, is Islamic property.

This rewriting of history has been going on for some years now. According to the new version there was no pre-Islamic occupation of the Temple Mount. In November 1999 and over a period of three days and three nights 12,000 tons of ancient archaeological remains was removed from the Temple Mount area and dumped in the Kidron valley in Jerusalem. A new mosque was recently built in the underground area known as Solomon's Stables. Israeli archaeological students have examined some of the remains found in the Kidron dumps and say that there is material from every archaeological period from the First temple to the time of the Ottoman empire.

Why have such ancient archaeological remains been removed in such haste and secrecy and without any proper archaeological supervision? The only answer is that the Muslim authorities do not want the world to know the true history of Israel, which lies below the surface of the Temple Mount. The rewriting of history is at the very heart of the conflict over Jerusalem.

The Palestinian mufti of Jerusalem, Sheikh Ikrima Sabri, told the German newspaper *Die Welt*:

> 'In the whole city, there is not even a single stone indicating Jewish history. Our right, on the other hand, is very clear. This place has belonged to us for 1,500 years.'

The Palestinians are deceiving the world into believing their false claims over the land of Israel. But the truth is this promised land was given by the God of Abraham, Isaac and Jacob, to the Jews who are the only people to have occupied this land continuously for the last 3,000 years.

It was this undeniable fact that caused all of Palestine to be given to the Jews in 1917 by the League of Nations as a national homeland. However, during the time of the British administration, the land was divided between Syria, Jordan and Lebanon, totally disregarding promises previously made to the Jewish people. Interestingly the decline of the British Empire dates back to this period in history. This land in which for 3,000 years there had been an unbroken Jewish presence, is now called by the media 'occupied territories'. The world has backed the Palestinian lie that states that they are the original owners of this land.

The acts of terrorism perpetrated against Israel and the US have been planned in order to rob Israel of her rightful inheritance so that Islam can gain full control of the Middle East.

Rewriting history is not new. Hitler did it, so did the Romans. In fact the title of Holy Roman Emperor has been handed down from one generation to another and for centuries was held by the former Imperial House of Austria/Hungary, the European Royal Family, the Habsburg Dynasty. This family also holds the title of King of Jerusalem granted in perpetuity after Jerusalem was taken from the Turks by the European crusaders. The Habsburgs retain the title to this day.

In 1899 Germany's Kaiser Wilhelm II began excavations of an ancient archaeological site in Babylon after visiting the Holy Land in his capacity as King of Jerusalem.

In 1913 he brought back parts of the Ishtar Gate, Babylon's symbol of Judenhass (hatred of Jews). It was housed in Berlin. Within five years Germany was at war. Ten million were dead. World War I had begun.

In the 1920s Liberal Theology was spreading like wild fire throughout Germany. The Bible was under dispute and was no longer believed to be the inspired Word of God.

In 1934 a reproduction of Satan's Seat or Pergamum's altar was erected in Nuremberg, providing a powerful and evil background for Hitler's Nazi rallies.

Hitler continued the archaeological excavations and the entire Processional Way, Babylon's Entrance to Hell, covered with the Snake Dragon god, was erected in Berlin.

The term 'anti-Semitism', or 'anti-Semitismus', invented by German journalist, Wilhelm Marr 1818–1904, and which was thought to be more respectable than the former Judenhass, or hatred of Jews, was just a new synonym for the old hatred. It was simply re-invented under a new disguise **The Third Reich**.

What's new?

1939–1945 World War II destroyed 55 million souls. Six million perished in the death camps of Nazi Germany, Hitler's *Final Solution* to the problem of the Jew. After Hitler's defeat in 1945 Pergamum's altar was carried away as booty to Leningrad. Fourteen years later it was returned to Berlin by Krushchev at the request of the German nation. It now stands in the Pergamum Museum in east Berlin and in 1999 Europe's Prime Ministers met in Germany's capital and Berlin was described by US President Clinton as '**the heart of a united Europe**'.

The *Mail on Sunday*, 13 May 2001 Headlines '**Europe Army H.Q. in Nazi Bunker**'.

The EU plan will mean the same tunnels and bomb-proof rooms used by the Nazi Luftwaffe Chief will be the command and control centre for the so-called Euro Army when it goes operational in 2003. The European Union Rapid Reaction Force will be run from the Nazi complex where Goering plotted Blitzkrieg on Britain.

Britain committed itself to the EU force in February 2001 as part of the Treaty of Nice. The British contingent is expected to include 24,000 troops.

At the time of writing this book in October 2001 Babylon's symbol of hatred towards the Jews and Satan's seat remain in Berlin, the capital city of Germany.

The world news page of the *Independent*, 7 November 2000, carried the headlines **'Conform or leave – Germany's Right tells immigrants. Yesterday the Christian Democrats declared "Foreigners are welcome in the Fatherland provided they behave just like Germans."'** They spoke of Patriotism, the Nation, the Fatherland and a new word 'Leitkultur' which critics say is an ill-disguised synonym for assimilation. This word was originally coined by an Arab political scientist. It means defining culture or prevailing culture. In a country where the holocaust is still a vivid memory, this has understandably provoked a furore.

According to Peter Muller, senior CDU politician in charge of drafting policy, 'Newcomers should learn German, respect the constitution and uphold the traditions of the land'. The latter he helpfully defines as,

> 'those formed by Humanism, the Enlightenment and Christianity.'

He goes on,

> 'for instance; immigrants should observe Sonntagfruhe, the rule of requiring all creatures living in Germany, even dogs, to make no noise on Sundays.'
>
> (*Independent*, 7 November 2001)

An eminent historian summed up anti Semitism as working in three stages:

1. You have no rights to live among us a Jews
2. You have no rights to live among us
3. You have no right to live.

> (*The Destruction of the European Jews*,
> Paul Hilberg)

Neo-Nazism is alive and well

Hitler believed he was a Messiah of a chosen race of people called Aryans, and that Jews were not only racially inferior, but were actually a menace poisoning the purity of Aryan blood.

The spirit of Neo-Nazism is alive and well and a frightening number of young Germans would welcome the Nazis back into power. A recent survey has found half of 14–16 year olds in the eastern part of Germany believe the Nazis have good points, and astonishingly, nearly one-sixth say the Nazi party itself was a good idea.

Interior Minister Otto Schilly admitted recently that 13,753 xenophobic and anti-Semitic crimes had been recorded in the year 2000, compared with 9,456 in 1999. The current rise in unemployment after the collapse of communism has created a **moral vacuum**, say the experts. Another recent survey showed how one-sixth of East Germans wish the communists were back in power.

Germany has only been a democratic country for 50 years. The ghosts of the communists and Nazis still run rampant and the ideals of Hitler and the Nazis, the perpetrators of the biggest mass slaughter in history, still holds allure for many youngsters in East Germany (*Daily Mail*, 8 February 2001).

Although Hitler's dream of a pure Aryan race who would rule the world did not come to pass, the demonic spirit behind this ideology is alive and well, and indeed it is dwelling among us, and many of its followers claim to have God on their side.

Martyrs of terror
Tidal waves of hatred are rising from the deep
From ancient grudges born of devilry
Lifting up their ugly heads their evil to repeat
They spew out curses old as history.

The murderous plans of these mendacious schemes
Rise from the ashes of the Holocaust
Death camps that reverberate,
With the sounds of human screams
Six million voices now reduced to dust.

The hatred of the Jew – *Judenhass*
Reveals its ugly anti-Semitic face –
Re-emerging like a snake in the grass
It strikes at any time and any place.

Past atrocities we never can undo
But it's our duty to unearth its evil root
Of the vitriolic, diabolic hatred of the Jew
And expose its vile contaminated fruit.

Today, six million voices are crying out aloud
They're warning us from their embittered sleep
That somewhere out there hiding in the crowd
Another neo-Nazi waits to leap.   (C. Wertheim)

German Propaganda against the Jews in World War II

'The Jew – the Inciter of War, the Prolonger of War'

Chapter 9

False Christs and False Prophets

Religious hatred

The enemy is in our midst. Jesus said,

> *'For false christs and false prophets will arise and show great signs and wonders, so as to deceive, if possible, even the elect.'*
> (Matthew 24:24)

The devil is behind the spirit of religiosity in all its shapes and forms. This is what false religion is, a shape or form of the truth, a copy of the original, a counterfeit.

> *'Pure and undefiled religion before God and the Father is this: to visit orphans and widows in their trouble, and to keep oneself unspotted from the world.'*
> (James 1:27)

Christian Identity churches have some estimated 30,000 followers in the USA alone. This religious cult was set up by an English man in the 1800s called Edward Hine. He taught that the tribe of Judah was Satan's creation. That same paranoia and hatred of Jewish people remains to this day. Christian Identity teaches a revised edition of Genesis. The basic concepts are as follows:

God made other humans of different skin colour as a test, or even a mistake, a trial-and-error experiment, however on the last day he got it right and made Adam and Eve, a white man and a white woman.

Identity followers believe that the Negro race was created to serve the white man. They even go so far as to say that all Jewish people and others of non-white origin, including all other minorities, are inferior and sub-human.

With these teachings solidly instilled in their minds, these so-called 'Christians' can act with a sense of righteousness, feeling fully justified as they commit acts of violence against so-called sub-species, even believing they are serving God, in the same way the Apostle Paul, or Saul, believed before his conversion when he was murdering Christians.

These teachings also underpinned much of Hitler's philosophy in *Mein Kampf* and represents an evil which confronts us in new and ever-more deadly forms to this very day.

Adolf Hitler believed in a unique race of people called Aryans, whose symbol was the sun or the four-armed Swastika. He believed a new breed of Nazi supermen could be produced who would destroy everybody on the planet who was not of pure Aryan descent.

Today in the mind of the suicide bomber is the concept of a glorious new Islamic world ruled by Allah. For this he will zealously die a martyr's death and become a hero in the eyes of his people and according to the Koran.

Paul's words bring it home to us:

> *'If anyone else thinks he may have confidence in the flesh, I more so: circumcised the eighth day, of the stock of Israel, of the tribe of Benjamin, a Hebrew of the Hebrews; concerning the law a Pharisee; concerning zeal, persecuting the church; concerning the righteousness which is in the law, blameless.'*

(Philippians 3:4–6)

Here he was stating clearly his mind-set before his conversion. He was a pure-blooded Jew, blameless according to the law, with a religious zeal that would stop at nothing, even the torture, persecution and death of his own people whom he believed were betraying God by following Jesus. This is the religious spirit behind all Holy Wars.

The current wave of violence, hatred and prejudice against the Jewish people has found its voice yet again through the Islamic word *Jihad*, which translated means 'Struggle'. It is interesting that *Mein Kampf*, Hitler's doctrine of the Third Reich, translated also means 'My Struggle'.

Is it not significant that the devil always imitates the things of God, producing the counterfeit, a copy of the original? What is God saying? It is not a coincidence that Israel also means 'to struggle with God'. Is this not a sign of this present age? Are we not in the time of 'Jacob's Trouble'?

> *'Alas! For that day is great,*
> *So that none is like it;*
> *And it is the time of Jacob's trouble,*
> *But he shall be saved out of it.'* (Jeremiah 30:7)

Do not be deceived

If all evidence of the Jews, i.e. historical and archaeological, were destroyed and all the biblical sites were to be re-invented under the names of false gods, then how could the Bible be true? And if the Bible records were falsified then the Gospel of Jesus the Messiah would simply be interpreted as nothing more than a legend or a myth.

There have been many recent reports of archaeologists and historians representing this current intellectual shift even in Israel itself. An emphasis on Jewish history is giving way to a more universal approach. Many are being deceived.

Universalism and humanism are among the many deceptions pervading Israel at this time. Sadly there are many from various backgrounds who are ready to bow the knee to yet another false god which is coming in the form of universalism and humanism. Not surprisingly the Palestinians are quick to capitalise.

People of this persuasion would choose to rewrite the Bible in terms of archaeology, the authority of 'science'. What stands in their way? The answer is God's people, the people of the Book. Jesus said,

> *'You worship what you do not know; we know what we worship,*
> *for salvation is of the Jews.'* (John 4:22)

Bloodstained history

President Bush's much-regretted reference to 'a crusade against terrorism' raised the nightmare prospect of fundamentalists getting their hands on nuclear weapons.

The headlines in the *Daily Mail*, 25 September 2001: 'Bin Laden's Battle Cry **"We ask God to make us defeat the infidels and to crush the new Jewish–Christian Crusader campaign that is led by the chief crusader Bush under the banner of the cross."** '

Powerful words bringing an echo of the past ringing out from the blood-stained pages of our history books, bringing to mind memories of the crusaders, only this time Jews and Christians are on the same side.

When Pope Urban II gave out his blood-curdling call to arms in 1095, his sermon established a creed which has served the interests of tyrants and dictators ever since. The Pope's sermon called upon all Christians to march upon the Turks, a Persian people who had overrun Jerusalem, and 'hasten to exterminate this vile race from our lands.' Many volunteered on the spot with cries of, 'God wills it.'

The march to Jerusalem began with massacres of the Jews in German cities. They entered Jerusalem on 15 July 1099. The carnage that followed was terrible, with piles of dead Muslims nearly as high as the houses, and the city's Jews who had taken refuge in the synagogues were burned alive, while the crusaders praised God in the church of the Holy Sepulchre in Jerusalem. Such is the zeal of the fanatic!

The messages of the crusades have echoed down the corridors of time and have been used again and again to serve the perpetrators of the Holocaust and modern ethnic cleansers in all their ghastly disguises.

The characters in this melodrama remain the same. Only God can break this eternal triangle between the Muslim, the Christian and the Jew.

Religion is the heart of the devil's plan to fool the world and bring deception into the church and upon the heads of the Jewish people and Israel.

The nature of the beast is war. He is tormented by his own megalomania, ravenous for power, deluded by his own lusts and desires. If he can inflict his torment upon us, so that his struggle becomes our struggle against each other, **Holy War**, then he will have won.

Chapter 10

Lest We Forget

Prince of Persia

In the Book of Esther we discover one of the earliest records of anti-Semitism. The Jews were exiled in the Persian Empire which then stretched over 120 provinces from India to Ethiopia. King Xerxes (486–465 BC) had three Royal seats, one was in Babylon (present-day Iraq) the others in Iran at Shushan and Hamadan. It is in Sushan, the winter capital, in South-west Iran, where the story of Queen Esther unfolds – the very place the Aryans are said to have originated.

Who are the Aryans? The *Oxford Dictionary* defines 'Aryan' as 'the ancient inhabitants of the Iranian plateau'.

The word 'Iran' is a modernised version of 'Aryan' and the *World Book Encyclopaedia* tells us 'Aryan' refers to a language spoken by a people who migrated from ancient Persia, some into Tibet and India, others into Germany and Europe.

The term 'Aryan' became linked with the theory of inferiority of certain races in the nineteenth century, at which time the terms Aryan and Semite became popular amongst the European intellectual elites.

In 1979 Iran became the world's largest theocracy. Islam is practised almost exclusively throughout this region.

Ayatollah Janate, a leading Moslem cleric in the Iranian government said, 'the 21st century will be the century for Islam.' The Koran says:

'Believers, take neither Jews nor Christians for your friends. They are friends of each other. Whoever of you seeks their friendship shall become one of their number. God does not guide the wrong doers.'

In the book of Daniel we are told of the Prince of Persia and the Prince of Greece and the spiritual conflict over the city of Jerusalem, the nation of Israel and the Jewish people.

Daniel had been praying and fasting for three weeks but opposing forces were at work holding things up. These demonic principalities came in the form of the Prince of the King of Persia. The Archangel Michael, believed to be the guardian angel of Israel and the Jewish people, came to the aid of the heavenly messenger, who is not named (Daniel 10:13–21; 12:1; Revelation 12:7).

The Princes of Persia and Greece are believed to be demonic principalities, having dominion over territories of the world, ideologies, cultures, the mind-sets of the nations, and the religious and political powers that rule them (Ephesians 6:12).

The Prince of Persia was the principality and power over the Persian Empire which covered most of the civilised world when Haman planned his *Jihad* against the Jewish people. The outcome was a near holocaust, followed by the salvation of the Jews through the prayers and actions of the Jewish Queen Esther.

Why remember Purim?

We are reminded to celebrate the two days of Purim (Esther 9:26–28) every year without fail, both Jew and Christian, all those that joined themselves with the Jewish people (verse 27), so that the memory of what almost happened in Persia should not perish.

Why does the Lord insist that we remember? Is it because Haman's followers are alive today?

Indeed in this very same location which is present-day Iran, the Iranian leadership seeks the total extermination of Israel, just as the Nazis did.

The territory of the Prince of Persia includes Iraq, Iran, Afghanistan and Saudi Arabia. Could this be the demonic power behind the terrorist attacks in New York and Washington, the evil mind-set behind the suicide bombers in the streets of Jerusalem and throughout Israel, the Prince of the air that is influencing the media against Israel, the vile and repugnant forces of darkness behind radical fanatic Islam?

In the book of Esther we read about Haman the Agagite who descended from the Amalekites, Israel's ancient enemies, whom God cursed, saying,

'You will blot out the remembrance of Amalek from under heaven.' (Deuteronomy 25:19)

Amalek was the grandson of Esau, who was the twin brother of Jacob whom God re-named Israel.

'Your name shall no longer be called Jacob, but Israel; for you have struggled with God and with men and have prevailed.'
(Genesis 32:28)

One of the names of Israel means 'He strives/struggles with God'.

In Romans 9:13 God says, *'Jacob* [or Israel] *I have loved, Esau I have hated.'* Esau abandoned his birthright for a pot of stew (see Genesis 25:31; Hebrews 12:16). In much the same way, many of the secular Jews in Israel and in the Diaspora would abandon Zion and hand it over to the Palestinian authority for the sake of 'Pie in the Sky' peace. They have been seduced by the gods of this world, a lesson to all of us.

The scars inflicted by hatred of the Jews still remain, and it's not surprising that Anti-Semitism is remembered at Purim, the Feast of Esther, when the Jewish children dress up as the biblical characters and make a lot of noise with football rattles, stamping their feet loudly after they have written the names of Haman and Hitler on the soles of their shoes.

During these two days in the synagogue the Megillah, 'The Scroll of Esther', will be read, also Exodus 17:8–16:

'Now Amalek came and fought with Israel in Rephidim. And Moses said to Joshua, "Choose us some men and go out, fight with Amalek. Tomorrow I will stand on top of the hill with the rod of God in my hand."

So Joshua did as Moses said to him, and fought with Amalek. And Moses, Aaron, and Hur went up to the top of the hill. And so it was, when Moses held up his hand, that Israel prevailed; and when he let down his hand, Amalek prevailed.

But Moses' hands became heavy; so they took a stone and put it under him, and he sat on it. And Aaron and Hur supported his hands, one on one side and the other on the other side; and his hands were steady with the going down of the sun.

So Joshua defeated Amalek and his people with the edge of the sword. Then the LORD *said to Moses, "Write this for a memorial in the book and recount it in the hearing of Joshua, that I* [the Almighty] *will utterly blot out the remembrance of Amalek from*

under heaven." And Moses built an altar and called its name The-
Lord-Is-My-Banner [or Miracle]; *for he said, "Because the Lord*
has sworn: the Lord will have war with Amalek from generation
to generation."'

We know that Haman was an Agagite descended from the
Amalekites, and during Purim the Jewish people are reminded
that **God Himself will have war with Amalek from generation
to generation**.

Signs of the times

The spirit of Amalek is still with us. In Numbers 24:20 we are
told,

> *'Amalek was first among the nations,*
> *But shall be last until he perishes.'*

The Rabbinical commentaries teach us that when Amalek is
referred to as, 'First among the nations but its end will be eternal
destruction', this means that Amalek represents the 'essence of
evil', a 'spiritual force' of evil against Israel, an 'eternal struggle'
of good versus evil. And, since that time has not yet come to
remove evil from the world, God did not permit Joshua to
destroy Amalek in Exodus 17, only to defeat him.

However, God has promised to utterly blot out the remembrance of Amalek from under heaven. The import is that the time
will come when evil will be utterly defeated and disappear when
Messiah comes (Rabbinical teachings).

Numbers 24:17 says,

> *'A Star shall come out of Jacob;*
> *A Sceptre shall rise out of Israel.'*

This is a Messianic prophecy to both Jews and Christians. The
Jewish people await His coming:

> *'I see Him, but not now;*
> *I behold Him, but not near.'*   (Numbers 24:17)

However, it is nearer than ever before in the history of this earth,
and the signs of the times speak for themselves.

The Rabbis tell us,

> 'When Messiah comes He will be like a shooting star or a meteor, because He will flash across the heavens visible to the whole world, to gather Jews from their dispersion, from wherever they are scattered.'

Jesus said,

> *'For as lightning that comes from the east is visible even in the west, so will be the coming of the Son of Man.'*
>
> (Matthew 24:27 NIV)

What do we tell them?
Civilisation...
Is under attack
Wealth
Peace
And Secularism
Deluded us into
A false sense of security
Concealing from us
The presence
Of the Abyss.

Now...
It has been exposed
Now
Our vulnerability is in full view
We live
In close proximity
To the end.

What do we tell
Our children?
Reared on fantasy
Called virtual reality
Hollywood movies
Computer games
Violence
Terror
False images.

Now the images are real
The dividing wall
Between truth and fiction
Has been blown apart
Like
The Twin Towers
This
Is Reality.

What do we tell our children?
Especially when
They see
Eleven year olds
Yelling their allegiance
To the jihad
Against the infidel
Willing to die
For their truth.

What do we tell them? ˋ
We tell them our truth
It's all we have!   (C. Wertheim)

Jesus said,

> *'I am the way, the truth, and the life.'*   (John 14:6)

Also,

> *'Train up a child in the way he should go,*
> *And when he is old he will not depart from it.'*   (Proverbs 22:6)

Chapter 11

What About the Children?

'Let the little children come unto Me, and do not forbid them;
for of such is the kingdom of God.'
(Mark 10:14)

12-year-old Mohammed-al-Durah

Child martyrs

The entire world has seen the pictures of Mohammed al Dura, the twelve-year old photographed while crouching beside his terrified father in the middle of an Israeli/Palestinian gun battle. The two were filmed cowering against a wall caught in the crossfire in which the boy was shot dead.

These famous pictures have become worldwide symbols used as propaganda against the so-called Israeli oppression of the Palestinians.

After lengthy investigations carried out by the Israeli military authorities it was concluded that the bullet which killed Mohammed was from a Palestinian gunman, but this did not make headline news.

Nor did a picture of a ten-month old baby girl, Shalherit Pass (meaning 'of Blessed Memory'), ever reach the Western media, yet she was deliberately murdered by a Palestinian sniper.

Who has heard of this little baby whose parents are religious Zionist settlers in Hebron? Who cares?

In this terrible battle where Palestinian children are trained to be child martyrs and babies are live targets, we are reminded of the words of Golda Meir, 'we will have peace with the Arabs when they love their children more than they hate us.'

> *'And you shall not let any of your descendants pass through the fire to Molech.'*   (Leviticus 18:21)

This is one of the lesser-known of the 613 commandments. You do not meet too many people these days that are performing this type of idol worship. Or do we?

This particular form of idol worship is child sacrifice and it has a unique aspect to it. It was only done in a situation where the individual would sacrifice only one and not all of his kids. This was done because the religious leader would assure the father that by sacrificing this child, it would benefit all the other children and they would be blessed and achieve success.

Afterwards, one could only imagine how the family and society must have revered this sacrificed child.

We can look at this part of the Bible and write it off as an expression of a sick, backward and primitive society that no longer exists. Yet upon closer inspection, and reading the recent news events, we see the truth in Solomon's words, *'There is nothing new under the sun.'* Is this practice any different from sending young children and teenagers into the heat of battle against heavily-armed Israeli soldiers, knowing full well there is the very real possibility of their death? They are martyred for the good of the greater society, killed to elicit world sympathy and assist those whom they leave behind. It is only the most depraved society that would commit such cruelty. What does it say about such mothers and fathers, and political leaders, who send their children to death and then turn them into noble warriors for the greater good?

How can Israel expect to forge a peace with a people who care so little for the life of their most innocent and precious commodities – their own children? If they display such inhumanity to their own – what can we expect of their treatment of us?

America and Jews all over the world must face the fact that we are not dealing with an ideology that shares our values of the preciousness of life (Rabbi Tzvi Nightingale, 25 October 2000).

Lies and more lies

The prince of the air spreads this obscene propaganda through the media, and Israel is always the loser. No amount of explanations will convince the world that Israel is not the 'Giant Goliath' against the vulnerable and small shepherd boy with only a stone and a sling, as the Palestinian and Arab media would have us believe. They are indeed masters at propaganda and the death of the twelve-year old Mohammed was used to justify the recent terrorist attacks on America as 'revenge' because of its support of Israel. Those Muslim clerics who support Osama Bin Laden would condone the killing of thousands in these acts, worthy of acclamation in Paradise.

Israel is a very small fish in a vast Islamic ocean of which the Palestinian cause is an integral part.

Some Muslim clerics in the West Bank and the Islamic world are already accusing Israel for the attacks on New York and Washington.

A convenient scapegoat

How easy it would be to once again point the finger of suspicion at the Jewish people, in the hope that they will be the scapegoat for a world that invented terrorism, that harboured terrorists, providing the very weapons and technological information, the tools of their trade, which they are now using against us.

How easy it would be to blame the Jewish people again for the atrocities of mankind, in the hope that evil will somehow be swept away and we can all go back to our fantasies and our computer games.

Mass hatred

Our newspapers, filled with pictures from Israel of suicide bombers, child martyrs and bus explosions, almost paled into insignificance beside the 'in your face' ferocity of the burning Twin Towers of the World Trade Centre as it crumbled to the ground.

If the power behind terrorism is media propaganda, then the terrorist attacks on New York and Washington have achieved a propaganda coup second to none in the history of modern terrorism.

What are we up against?

The *Daily Mail*, 12 September 2001:

'To begin to comprehend it you have to be aware of the greatest mass hatred in the modern world, that of millions throughout the Arab and larger Muslim world against the State of Israel, and against their overwhelmingly most important backers, the Americans.'

If you need evidence of this you need only look at the TV pictures of the Palestinians dancing in the streets of Jerusalem to celebrate.

What is the answer to this hatred?

Prime Minister Tony Blair called it 'the new evil in our world today,' fanatics utterly indifferent to the sanctity of life.

These terrorists have sold their souls to the devil and the nature of the beast is death, destruction, suicide and murder.

Out of the mouths of babes

'In that hour Jesus rejoiced in the Spirit and said, "I praise You, Father, Lord of heaven and earth, that You have hidden these things from the wise and prudent and revealed them to babes. Even so, Father, for so it seemed good in Your sight.' (Luke 10:21)

About two weeks before all hell broke loose in America, Israel watched in amazement as an eight-year-old girl, whose mother and father and three siblings were blown up just days before in front of her eyes, and whose own body was covered in burns, told a TV interviewer:

> ' "I want to say that even though I am injured and everyone was injured, one must know that it is all from God, who wants us to behave better. In a little while the Messiah will come and whoever is dead and passed away in wars or the Arabs have killed him, he will come back to life, and then I will meet dad and mom and everyone."
>
> No-one was left to tutor her in what to say. Her pure faith came from within, the same pure faith that enabled her father Mordechai Schijveschuurder, to tell his wife and children to recite the Shema Israel prayer as their lives ebbed away. The role she was assigned was not one any of us would choose. She was given a solo, she played it sublimely. She revealed the potential for holiness with which each of us was created.' ('In good faith', Jonathan Rosenblum, *International Jerusalem Post*, 14 September 2001)

Chapter 12

A War of Two Worlds

Whose side are we on?

The world is growing darker by the minute. As it was at the beginning of creation, so it is now. God is separating the light from the darkness, the contrasts are becoming more extreme and the distinction between the two more obvious. There are no more grey areas, no room for compromise.

The world is in a war against terrorism. World War III will be unlike any war that has ever been, or ever will be again. It may be the war to end all wars.

The distinction between the two powers that oppose one another in this conflict are becoming more obvious and the vast area of **no man's land** in between more inhospitable.

The time is coming upon us faster than we think, when the middleman who sits (albeit precariously) on his fence, must either stand or fall on one side or the other. '**If we don't stand for something we will fall for anything**', and in this case it is knowing whose side we are on that is going to make the difference.

A world of extremes

It is hard for any modern European to sit back and watch the atrocities that have taken place recently and not glimpse our own dark shadows.

It has been said that 11 September marks the end of one era and the start of another. This is a war with a difference because we will never know who is on the winning side. There will be no victors, no VE Day to celebrate our triumph, no conclusion, no answer, no gain. The terror within our midst is invisible like a snake in the grass, and we have given it the freedom and provided the ammunition for it to strike at any time, anywhere in this so-called 'free world'.

This is a world of extremes: in the West freedom has been taken to the nth degree. Women walk around half-naked, sex and drugs and rock 'n' roll are the words that have echoed down the generations since the post-war revolution and the contraceptive pill came into being. In the Muslim Fundamentalist nations such as Iran and Afghanistan, the pendulum has swung in the opposite direction. Women are so overpowered and hidden from view they are fortunate if they can peer out at the world through a slit in the veil. It's almost as if the pendulum is swinging so fast and so wide that our focus has become blurred and the two opposing forces have become one.

'The truth shall make you free' (John 8:32)

'The world has gone mad today, good's bad today, black's white today, day's night today.'

These are the words of Cole Porter, and they are prophetic. Written at the beginning of the last century they heralded in another **new era**, an era of so-called freedom where anything goes. Irving Berlin, a Russian-born Jew, whose real name was Israel Baline, also wrote his song 'God bless America' in 1917, published in 1939, which has been sung again recently and these words have been used as the finishing lines to President Bush's speeches over and over again. We too echo that prayer 'God bless America' and the free democratic nations, and help us to use this freedom to honour our God whom we need now more than ever before.

Muslims who want peace

Many Muslims want to live in peace and believe Islam to be a religion of love and peace. Islam and Christianity share the same Jewish roots and the Arabs are among the kindest and most hospitable people on earth. There are also some biblical truths to be found in Islam. However, the fact is that Islam has led many millions of otherwise peace-loving peoples into gross deception.

The teaching of the Koran, blended together with the ancient grudges recorded in the Bible dating back to Isaac and Ishmael,

Esau and Jacob, and leading up to the more recent Church history of the crusades, provide ample fuel to incite the hatred of the Arab against Israel and the Church.

Islam, at its most fanatical level, is revealing its true face, and it stands in direct opposition to God's Word, and God's people – the people of the Book, both Jews and Christians.

What is *Jihad*?

If we are in a war then the nature of this war needs to be understood. The newspapers speak of *Jihad* (Islam's Holy War).

Jihad is quite different from traditional wars. *Jihad* is a continuous state of war against the infidel until all nations bow the knee to Allah.

War, as we understand it in the West, is a means to an end, whether it is waged for ambition or self-interest or for religious purposes, where the **normal** situation is peace between the peoples. From a Western perspective war constitutes a dramatic event which must end in a return to peace.

In Islam the **normal** situation is war, eternal war. To a Muslim the concept of peace can only be in a Muslim world between Muslim and Muslim. Periods of ceasefire are used only as a tactical choice, if and when the enemy is too strong, and only for a period of time, never longer than ten years.

From a Muslim perspective agreements are also part and parcel of the strategies of war. Benjamin Netanyahu understood the Arab mind-set when he wrote twenty years ago,

> 'Agreements are not there to be kept, only to get advantage for the continuation of war.'

Any territory conquered by Islam cannot be de-Islamised. No matter who takes it, it will always remain 'occupied territory'. Islam is territorial by nature and Jerusalem which was once under Islamic rule, to the mind of the Muslim, will always remain their territory. War is eternal, a given thing in Islam, and every soldier who dies while fighting the 'infidel' dies a martyr. There is no other sure way of entering paradise than through dying a martyr's death.

Jihad means 'to struggle in the cause of Allah with pen, speech or sword'. Infiltration is yet another strategy of Islamic war. The destruction of the Twin Towers was an **inside job**. America was attacked on its own land, a concept alien to the Western mentality. This is a war of **existence**, one mind-set against another – East and West.

Jihad is a religious duty, an obligation, one of many duties and obligations the Muslim **must** fulfil. In the Koran *Jihad* is repeatedly mentioned. It is at the heart of the religious message and is the **best way** the believer can obey it. The references to *Jihad* make it quite clear that it is **not** a spiritual war. It is a military battle and *Jihad* is Islam's **normal** strategy and traditional means of exposition. It is an intrinsic part of the Islamic faith and institution. In fact *Jihad* is the institution which binds all others collectively into this religious ideology.

War is the condition of all life; to live is to be at war. Wars within the Muslim world are numerous. From the Muslim's perspective, peace with this world is impossible. There are only two domains – the *dar al ilam* and the *dar al harb* – the Domain of Islam and the Domain of War.

In *Jihad* there are no victors and no vanquished, only the world of Islam and the world of war. In the Islamic mind-set there is only total submission to Allah.

How can you bomb an ideology?

Today we are faced with a global impact of intellectual terrorism. This is the modern face of Islam. To this war there is no end.

The resurgence of the traditional policy of Islam has been going on since the revolution of Islam in Iran in 1979, an event which has been compared in importance to the French and Bolshevik revolutions by Sir Anthony Parsons, Britain's last Ambassador to the Shah of Persia who said, 'The Islamic fundamentalists are the Bolsheviks of our time.'

The fanatical leader of Iran, the late Ayatollah Khomeini who ousted the Shah and brought a resurgence of Islamic fundamentalism to the Middle East, preached,

> 'The purest joy in Islam is to kill and be killed for Allah.'
> (Shorrosh, *Islam Revealed*, p. 35)

Iranian Ayatollah Fazl, Allah Mahalati writes,

> 'He who takes up a gun, a dagger, a kitchen knife or even a pebble with which to harm and kill the enemies of the faith has his place assured in heaven. An Islamic State is a state of

war until the whole world sees and accepts the light of the True Faith.'   (*Ibid*)

Willing, dedicated, unscrupulous in their methods, convinced of their righteousness, the Iranian revolution provided the inspiration, the spark necessary to revive Islamic Imperialism and to recall its true nature which is fundamentally war-like. The global movement of Islamic fundamentalism that spread after 1979 reveals its true face. The goal is nothing less than the world.

Chapter 13

Obedience to Mohammed

Death to the moderate

While moderate Muslims reject terrorism, all Islamic scholars agree that terrorists act in direct obedience to Mohammed, the Koran, Allah and Islam.

The torture and slaughter of millions in Southern Sudan and Indonesia is the result of Islamic violence which is the duty of every Muslim in order to spread Islam until it takes over the whole earth.

Any moderate Muslim who rejects this ideology does so at the risk of his life. Tens of thousands of Muslim Arabs were slaughtered in the Wars of Apostasy shortly after Mohammed's death, when many Arabians believed they could free themselves from Islam. From then on Islam was spread everywhere with the sword.

Islam, in itself, is a religion based on terror, and its followers are not extremists or fanatics as we in the West would understand these terms, but sincere followers of Mohammed, and although suicide is forbidden, to sacrifice one's life in *Jihad* carries the highest reward.

Islam has no assurance of forgiveness except through martyrdom in holy war. The martyr is promised seven rewards:

1. Forgiveness of all sins
2. A reserved place in Paradise
3. Crowned in glory
4. Seventy-two virgins
5. Spared the suffering of the grave
6. Spared Judgement Day
7. Seventy relatives to accompany him in Paradise

Many moderate Muslims would say these promises have been taken and quoted out of context. They are nevertheless there to be applied and are being used to train terrorists.

There is a debate going on in the Islamic world over whether the attack on the World Trade Centre on 11 September came under the category of Holy War. For the criminals concerned, it did.

Osama Bin Laden and his Al-Qaeda organisation can be likened to the Ismaeli sect known as the Assassins, led by Hassan Sabbah in the eleventh century in the mountainous regions of Northwest Iran. Their leader had a Messianic vision like the Al Qaeda's adherence. They wrote,

> 'We must act in public as an example ... by killing one man we terrorise one hundred thousand. However it is not enough to die, for if by killing we discourage our enemies from undertaking any action against us, by dying in the most courageous fashion, we force the masses to admire us and from their midst men will come to join us. Dying is more important than killing. We kill to defend ourselves, but we die to convert and conquer.'

The Assassins derived their name from the Arabic word *Hash-shashin* (meaning 'smokers of hashish'). The drug was used to stir up passions before terrorising their victims. The same methods are being used today to brainwash young, Islamic fundamentalists into the mindless fanaticism of Holy War.

There are **moderate** Muslims but there is no such thing as **moderate** Islam.

Christian massacre

In Indonesia white-robed killers, carrying the Koran and chanting Islamic prayers, murdered Christians, burning down their villages, raping, beating and shooting their victims.

In Maluk, Eastern Indonesia, at least 10,000 Christians have been murdered by Islamic extremists. A further 8,000 Christians men, women and children, have been forced to convert to Islam and undergo circumcision in the most horrific conditions. Nearly half a million Christians are enduring appalling suffering as refugees. They have been pressurised by the government to return to their villages but the Islamic extremists group, Laskar Jihad, has declared that Christians cannot go back to 'cleansed' areas unless they convert to Islam.

In the Central Sulawese province a 3,000-strong Jihad army is closing in on Christians holed-up in the town of Tentena.

A pastor said, 'If we do not get help soon, thousands of Christians will cease to exist by the year end.'

How much longer will appeals for international intervention go unheeded and the press remain silent? How much longer will we stand by and do nothing when we hear our brothers' blood crying out to us from the ground? (Genesis 4:10).

In the city of Jos, northern Nigeria, people were being burned alive in Christian/Muslim violence. On 9 September 2001 at least 50 Nigerians were feared dead. Churches and mosques were set on fire.

The rise of Islam

Islam is a civilisation. It is not a religion based on articles of faith. It has a legal system which is unique, engulfed by rules of behaviour set in the Koran.

Islam is an autocracy, both malevolent and benevolent in which there is no separation between religion and politics. All are combined in the Koran.

This civilisation was once the greatest empire on earth, with government, laws, economy, language, architecture, music and literature. It is preparing to rise again. Wherever you have Islam, you will have war.

Christian political power and the land of Israel are the main obstacles to the army of Islam. This is a war of existence, one civilisation against another.

There are more Jewish people in New York than in Israel. They represent an influential lobby, a pressure group. America depends on the vote of this large Jewish contingent. There is an equally large, if not larger, Christian contingent of evangelical believers in America, who are Zionists and who fervently believe that the land of Israel belongs to the Jewish people.

At the Durban conference on Racism the fifty-five Muslim Bloc Nations made a defiant stand against Israel, branding the Israeli nation as an apartheid state guilty of ethnic cleansing and genocide. Both Israeli and Jewish delegates were subjected to racial abuse and physical harassment ... What hypocrisy!

The contradictions were apparent when after the accusations of Israeli wickedness, Western debauchery and the grave sin of Islamophobia, one of the delegates Suhir Mostafa, a Moroccan from a strictly observant Muslim state, was tempted to enjoy

Durban's raunchy night life. His pleasures however, were short lived. In the morning his body was found under the bed. He had been poisoned.

'For the word of God is living and powerful,
and sharper than any two-edged sword,
piercing even to the division of soul and spirit,
and of joints and marrow,
and is a discerner of the thoughts and intents of the heart.'
(Hebrews 4:12)

Chapter 14

We Are Being Warned

Self-righteous indifference

The world is at war, not *Jihad* or Holy war, not even against terrorism. Aren't we all guilty of feeding this monster by our own self-righteous indifference to the condition of our own souls? We are at war at every level of society in both East and West, whether it be road rage or child abuse, rape or murder. The list of heinous crimes fills our newspapers.

Whether it was in the Killing Fields of Cambodia, Bosnia or East Timor, the Armenian Massacre or the Holocaust, it has been said the last century was the most violent in the history of mankind, with over 50 million murdered.

What will the statistics on murder be in this century? Will there be anyone left to write them down?

The world is at war, but *Jihad* is not the answer. Like all religion, Islam is in conflict within itself. For us, who are in the world but not of it, our weapons are not carnal but spiritual.

> *'For we wrestle not against flesh and blood, but against principalities, against powers, against the rulers of the darkness of this world, against spiritual wickedness in high places.'*
>
> (Ephesians 6:12 AV)

Are we listening?

We are living in a time when the significance of world events can only be fully interpreted by Scripture. We are being confronted by the truth of God's Word as we witness God's judgements being loosed upon the earth in ever-increasing intensity. They are warnings to the Church, to world governments, to the man in the street ... to turn back to the God of the Bible before it's too late.

The British promised to recreate a homeland for the Jewish people which was to become Mandate Palestine, on both sides of the River Jordan. However, this never came to pass and the land ended up by being divided and given to the Arabs. Three-quarters of Mandate Palestine forms what we now know as the Kingdom of Jordan.

The hope was that this would be the final settlement of the land conflict between Arabs and Jews. Seeking future alliances with the huge Arab empire, Britain continued to fan the flames of conflict between Arabs and Jews.

In 1948 Britain armed and trained large Arab armies before withdrawing from Western Palestine. The expectation was that the Jews would be annihilated. However, in the war that followed God was with Israel and her enemies were defeated.

The fact is that the British reneged on their promises to the Jews. The question is whether successive British governments ever had any intention of creating a Jewish state, even though under the UN Mandate for this area they were obligated to do so.

If Britain continues with her current policy toward Israel and if we in the West continue to flout the biblical laws that all democratic nations once stood for, then we will be bringing God's wrath upon our own heads.

> *'I call heaven and earth as witnesses today against you, that I have set before you life and death, blessing and cursing; therefore choose life, that both you and your descendants may live.'*
>
> (Deuteronomy 30:19)

Those who choose death will bring upon themselves the most tragic of all the biblical verses, namely Revelation 20:15:

> *'And anyone not found written in the Book of Life was cast into the lake of fire.'*

The decadent West

There is an old Indian proverb that carries a message of truth which we could apply today to the present conflict between East and West:

'Never judge a man until you've walked one moon [one month] wearing his moccasins.'

How do we, the Western democratic nations, including Israel (the only democracy in the Middle East) appear to the eyes of the Muslims? **To them, we represent the people of the Book, the Christians and Jews.**

Do we represent the God of Abraham, Isaac and Jacob bringing glory to His Holy Name? Do we follow Jesus who said, *'I am the way, the truth, and the life. No one comes to the Father except through Me'* (John 14:6), and whose life upheld the Word of God, fulfilling the holy laws, living in the truth of the Almighty in thought, word and deed?

Have we profaned the Holy Scriptures with our compromise over such issues as abortion, homosexuality, child abuse, pornography, violence, perversion, fornication and divorce? The list, goes on and on ... and in the realms of medical science are we not **playing at being God** as we progress in areas such as cloning and other forms of genetic engineering?

Germ warfare

Islam is not entirely wrong when it accuses us of being decadent and filled with iniquity. Even biological germ warfare is an evil we in the West are as guilty of as anyone else, and we should not be surprised (as we have been warned for years that the danger of germ-based terrorism is inevitable), now that we are virtually defenceless against a bio-attack.

Who is responsible for this evil? In the 1950s a programme was established at Fort Detrick, near Washington, where bacteria and viruses were developed for use against America's enemies.

However, there is nothing new under the heavens. More than two millennia ago the Bible recounted how Scythian archers had dipped arrowheads in manure and rotting corpses to increase the deadliness of the wounds caused by them.

In the fourteenth century Tartars hurled plague-ridden corpses over the walls of enemy cities. In the eighteenth and nine-teenth centuries British soldiers gave blankets contaminated with smallpox to hostile tribes. In World War II the Japanese killed thousands by dropping fleas infected with plague on Chinese cities.

Is there no limit to man's imagination when it comes to war?

A global, moral community?

Out of the 40 poorest countries in the world, 24 are in the midst of armed combat or have just emerged from it. Africa is one example. Tens of millions, at least half being children, and 90% non-combatants, have been murdered as a result of war. The weapons used to fight these wars are overwhelmingly supplied by Britain and the US.

The biggest arms exporters in the world are also the two leaders in the war against terrorism. One-fifth of the world's arms sales come from Britain, a third of which goes to 'dubious countries'. Half of these go to the Middle East.

In the year 2000 Britain subsidised the arms trade to the tune of £420 million. Are we prepared to set an example in this New World Order quoted so often in the newspapers and in the media of a **Global Moral Community**?

In global capitalism of the nineteenth century, the top 20% of the world enjoyed three times as much income as the bottom 20%.

Today, in 2001, the top 20% creams off 86% of world income, the bottom 20% manage on only 1%. Much of the massive debts burdening the poorest nations are due to unpaid arms bills.

Are we prepared to risk our arms sales? Our financial free-wheeling every day is between $1.5 trillion and $2 trillion, mostly speculative.

Chapter 15

Who Owns the Media?

A Western mind-set

The Western media is the deciding factor in terms of world information, manipulating the masses by dictating what will inevitably result in its reaction and judgement to what the media chooses to reveal.

Three of the four major TV and radio networks, 59 magazines including *Time* and *Newsweek*, 58 newspapers including the *New York Times*, *The Washington Post* and the *Los Angeles Times* are controlled by ten financial and business corporations.

Ninety per cent of the world's press, TV and radio, is supplied by four Western news agencies. More than two-thirds of their correspondents are based in the West. The West exports over half of all TV programmes into Asia. During the Gulf War in 1991, CNN provided the news to both President Bush and Saddam Hussein.

Synergy

The maximising of profits through industrial expansion: most of the media output is controlled by only a handful of media conglomerates.

> 'In the normal hiring and firing of reporters, editors, writers and producers, the owning corporations quietly eliminate those who do not conform to corporate wishes. Anyone who believes that writers have complete freedom also believe in the tooth fairy.'
>
> ('Foreign Media Dance to Piper-Payers Tune', *Jerusalem Post*, 4 September 1992)

Some corporate owners intervene directly to control the news and public information. Controlling the viewers' perception of events is an old trick and was used in Nazi Germany. 1,400 anti-Semitic propaganda films were produced between 1939–1945 leading up to the death of six million Jews in the Nazi death camps.

Oil control

The West remains vulnerable to blackmail as long as the world is dependent upon Middle Eastern oil.

Prices will skyrocket as oil supplies inevitably decrease, and the cost of extraction increases. Whose side will the West be on?

Oil representatives sit on the boards of the most powerful news media. One single conglomerate owns the world's seven largest oil companies, one of which is Standard Oil of New Jersey, Exxon, which in turn controls 321 other oil companies, some of which are the largest corporations in the world.

The Council on Foreign Relations and the Tri-Lateral Commission (which actually run the US Government), is also under their control, plus every facet of the information industry, from TV to public education. This single conglomerate is the Rockefeller family. John Davison Rockefeller, 1839–1937, the founder of Standard Oil in 1870, controlled 90% of US refineries by 1882. He also founded the Rockefeller Foundation in 1913.

Arab and Iranian oil owners control the other two-thirds of the world's supply. The freedom of the press belongs to those who own one.

The pressure on world governments through the petro-dollar is one and the same as that which brings economic and political bias against Israel.

In a world economy dictated by the power of oil Israel will always be expendable. The facts speak for themselves.

Western advertising

It has been said that news is what someone, somewhere wants to suppress. All the rest is advertising.

Most individuals in the West have read, seen or heard 50 million advertisements by the time they reach 50 years of age.

Even presidential/parliamentary elections are now determined by advertising backed by vast amounts of money.

Advertising is aimed solely at making an emotional impact.

In the West, beauty is big business.
The 'cosmetic industry' brings in more money
than the 'arms trade'.

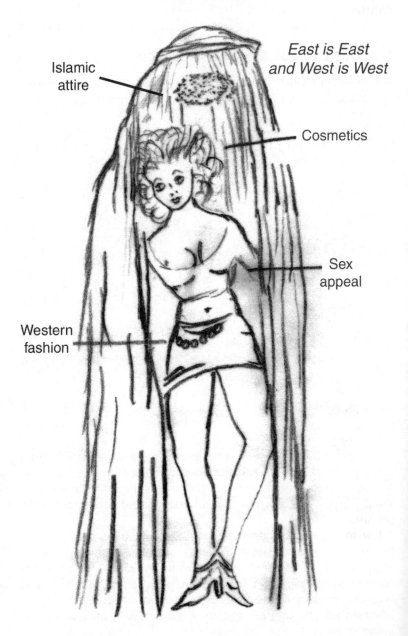

East is East
and West is West

Islamic
attire

Cosmetics

Sex
appeal

Western
fashion

Sensational news features are produced in various ways. Sex and violence are potent forces used by the media. TV presenters and newscasters are often chosen for their looks rather than their abilities.

The business of sex and violence

The Western representation of the female dictated by the post-modern culture has a long history. It's still used in all forms of advertising.

Whether semi-naked or laced and corseted, the female form has been degraded and exploited for purposes of power over the male since time immemorial. Sex has now become an integral part of Western advertising in the media.

Violence is another 'best-seller' in the media world and war correspondents can become 'celebrities' overnight.

Established facts are filtered through chosen political channels, setting the agenda on which issues are discussed.

Even world leaders are manipulated by the news media, which has unashamedly been known to stage-direct scenes of violent protest, deliberately misleading the public and politicians alike. Scenes and events can be manipulated through subliminal pictures, sound effects, lighting and background. Massive salaries and immense power is wielded by the top brass in the media who often earn as much as Hollywood stars, and their ability to influence world governments is overwhelming.

Egyptian media

Since the 1979 declaration of peace between Israel and Egypt, anti-Semitic images have continued to thrive. In the Egyptian media, over the last 20 years, regardless of the political climate, the derogatory Nazi symbols and harsh accusations against Jews prevail.

Jewish people are portrayed as dirty, hook-nosed, money-hungry, world-dominators. Echoes of *The Protocols of the Elders of Zion* persist. Articles on Holocaust denial, and cartoons depicting the Israeli government as evil through the use of Nazi symbols, shape popular opinion throughout the region of the Middle East, through the export of newspapers, magazines and books.

Brainwashed to hate

Egypt is the intellectual hub of the Arab world and is influencing an entire generation who have come of age since the 1979 peace treaty. Men, women and children are constantly exposed to these negative presentations of Jewish people as demons and murderers, a people to be avoided and feared.

Jewish people are displayed as sub-human equal with Nazis. Illustrations of Israeli leaders wearing swastikas and cartoons of Ehud Barak and Ariel Sharon dressed in Nazi uniform with a superimposed Hitler moustache label the Jews as being militant and brutal.

The purpose is to incite hatred and to remove any credibility of Israel's hope and intention to live at peace with its Arab neighbours. On the contrary the message in these anti-Semitic caricatures invoke stereotypes of the Jew as cunning, dangerous, wicked and opposed to peace. It promotes the lie that the Israelis enjoy killing innocent Arabs.

Many cartoons depict Israelis/Jews controlling the American government, which may have contributed to the false rumour that John Davison Rockefeller was a Jew.

The evil powers behind the Egyptian media affect Muslim men, women and children, many of whom have never met a Jew, and know no better than to believe the fake, fraudulent and biased reports against Israel.

Jews depicted as Nazis in Egyptian media

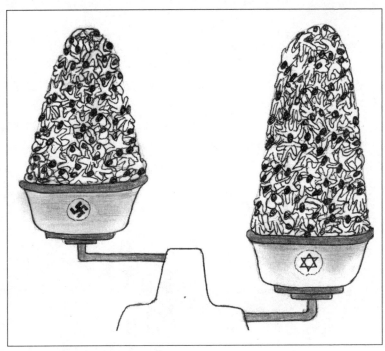

Memories of the Holocaust. Anti-Semitic propaganda against Israel

Ancient grudges – born of devilry

Chapter 16

What Time Is It?

A time to prepare

The Greeks had two words for time – *chronos*, which is the time we tell by clock or calendar and *kairos*, which is the **opportune time**, and the **destined time**. What we do in the *chronos* time will prepare us for the *kairos* time.

We are told,

> *'See then that you walk circumspectly, not as fools but as wise, redeeming the time because the days are evil.'*
>
> (Ephesians 5:15–16)

The Bible is warning us to be aware of what is going on around us, to have spiritual eyes to see from all angles, then, and only then will we see the whole picture.

God sees everything from beginning to end. In the vision of Ezekiel he describes intersecting wheels full of eyes (Ezekiel 1:16–20). Spiritual eyes can see all around. What we do in one area of our life will affect us in another. We, the Church, must stand with Israel in this her time of need.

The *kairos* time is coming upon us fast. The time of our destiny is closer than we think.

Now in the *chronos* time we must prepare for the time that lies ahead. We must *'pray for the peace of Jerusalem'* (Psalm 122:6).

We fight our battles in the Spirit before they happen. God will protect us. He has a plan for our lives, and for the world, but the enemy of our soul has a plan too.

Deliver us from evil

A number of years ago on one of my frequent trips to Jerusalem I was walking with a friend from the Temple Mount to our hostel on the Mount of Olives.

For reasons which at the time I did not understand (now I know that God had caused it for our protection), I was overcome with the Spirit of prayer. I could not be silent. My friend was perturbed at this extreme behaviour, thinking I was being most unsociable, however, in spite of her complaints nothing could silence me. In fact the urge to pray loudly in the Spirit was growing stronger by the minute.

As we approached the hostel, in a quiet road close to one of the Arab villages, we were accosted by four Arab youths who, seeing that we were tourists (especially my friend who is blonde and was attractively-dressed in a style typical of the West), began to assault us and throw stones.

I continued in prayer, only now even louder, looking straight into the eyes of our attackers, who amazingly enough turned and fled. A few minutes later some Arab children, who had been watching from the side of the road, asked me where I had learned Arabic, as that was the language of my prayer.

To this day I do not know what I shouted at those youths which caused them to run away in such fear. All I know is the Lord had prepared me in the *chronos* time, while I was walking with my friend, for the *kairos* time which only He could have known would come upon us. That prayer may well have saved our lives.

1 Corinthians 14:22:

> *'Therefore tongues are for a sign, not to those who believe but to unbelievers ... '*

Acts 2:8:

> *'And how is it that we hear, each in our own language in which we were born?'*

Write the vision

Habakkuk was the last prophet in Judah before the destruction of Jerusalem. He lived in *chronos* time about 600 BC, between the fall of Nineveh and the fall of Jerusalem.

Judah was filled with violence and corruption, the poor were under oppression and everywhere there was immorality and debauchery. The wicked had risen to power and were prospering at the expense of the poor and righteous. Habakkuk did not have a TV or newspapers like we do today, but he saw what was going on around him and was troubled. In his distress he cried out to God for an answer as to why the wicked continued to go unpunished. He received his answer in a vision.

Today we see a similar scene on our TV screens. We see the suffering of helpless old men, women and children all over the world, caught up in the endless cycle of famine, drought, poverty and war, while others live in luxury and amass great wealth.

Today, as in the time of Habakkuk, Jerusalem is centre stage.

> 'Is it just that the Jews are news or because wealthy oil states, and three major religions play a part in the Arab/ Israeli conflict?'
>
> (*Holy War for the Promised Land* – David Dolan)

In Habakkuk's day the enemy was Babylon. Isn't it the same today?

> '*MYSTERY, BABYLON THE GREAT,*
> *THE MOTHER OF HARLOTS*
> *AND THE ABOMINATION OF THE EARTH.*'
>
> (Revelation 17:5)

This is *chronos* time! Self, pleasure and power, the ugliness of spiritual adultery and unfaithfulness are behind the corruption of this present world system.

But we fight the battles in the Spirit **before** they happen. *Kairos* time will come upon us. We are being warned.

Habakkuk was told to write the vision down:

> 'Then the LORD *answered me and said:*
> "*Write the vision*
> *And make it plain on tablets,*
> *That he may run who reads it.*
> *For the vision is yet for an appointed time;*
> *But at the end it will speak, and it will not lie.*
> *Though it tarries, wait for it;*
> *Because it will surely come,*
> *It will not tarry.*'
>
> (Habakkuk 2:2–3)

One day the sickening scenes on my television screen of the continued violence and suffering worldwide – the result of man's inhumanity to man, caused me to cry out to the Lord in prayer. The Lord answered me and said ... 'Write the vision down.'

Habakkuk 2001
Adonai, Adonai,
When will you hear your servant's cry?
Great film director in the sky
Reach out Your mighty hand
This movie must be banned.

As the camera keeps on turning
Pillage and cruelty prevail
Towns and villages are burning
Homeless people weep and wail.

Armies march across the lands
Fiercer than wolves at night
Doing dreadful deeds with bloodstained hands
Deluded by their power and might.

Evil despots filled with greed
Throw out dragnets, haul in wealth
Fly like vultures to their feed
Worshipping the god of self.

Violence fills the very air
Lawlessness rules men with fear
Orphaned children stand and stare
The earth is soaked with human tears.

Disturbing visions fill our screens
Of ruins where twin towers stood
Shattered lives and broken dreams
Lie in the rubble, stained with blood.

If only we could just rewind
This reel of film and pause awhile
Rethink, rewrite the script and find
An ending that would make us smile.

O Adonai, You are the One
Who wrote the script for us to read
You warned us that these times would come
Hearts would grow faint and flesh would bleed.

The Bible written long ago
The Word of God the prophets spoke
Remind us that we need to know
The just shall live by faith and hope.

The vision on our movie screens
Is live ... this is the appointed time
The closing act, the final scenes
Speak of the end, they do not lie.

The final scene about to play
Will surely come without delay
O Adonai reach out your hand
This movie must be banned.

(C. Wertheim)

'Lift up your eyes to the heavens
And look upon the earth beneath.
For the heavens shall vanish away like smoke,
The earth will grow old like a garment,
And those who dwell in it will die in like manner;
But My salvation shall be forever,
And My righteousness will not be abolished.'

(Isaiah 51:6)

'For behold I create new heavens and a new earth;
And the former shall not be remembered or come to mind.'

(Isaiah 65:17)

Back to the Prince of Persia

Iran has always been uncompromising about Israel's **right to exist** and in December 2000 former President Hashema Rafsanjani implied that Israel could be the target of an Islamic nuclear attack. Iran's recent alliance with the Palestinian Authority over the cache of arms found aboard the *Karine* – a ship captured in the Red Sea by the Israelis on 4 January 2002, which was loaded off the Iranian coast – has made her Israel's number one enemy.

Iran has developed ties with Palestinian radical groups such as Islamic Jihad and Hamas. All accept Islamic fundamentalism, all are idealogical and religious and all are radically anti-Oslo. Iran is closer to the Islamic Jihad than any other foreign organisation other than Hezbullah. What they are offering the Palestinians is the Lebanonization of the territories. They used Hezbullah from Lebanon, but that was not enough, they want Jerusalem.

Experts emphasise that the dangers created by the alliance are still minor, compared to the existential threat posed by the possibility of Iran gaining nuclear arms. This would be far worse than the Palestinian problem, however, it is unclear as to when Iran's nuclear programme will come to fruition.

US President George W. Bush, on hearing reports that some of Osama Bin Laden's followers had crossed from Afghanistan into Iran, which shares a thousand kilometre border, responded harshly, 'Iran must be a contributor in the war against terror.'

Both Iran and Iraq have hidden many of their nuclear facilities underground, having leaned the lessons from the Iraqi Osirak nuclear reactor bombing by Israel in June 1981.

A confrontation between Israel and Iran could be dangerous in the event that Iran completed its nuclear programme.

Iran can attack Israel directly within minutes through Hezbullah in Southern Lebanon. Israel is limited by the need to travel 1,200 kilometres to attack Iran. Israel must do **everything** to counter that danger (Excerpts from *International Jerusalem Post*, 25 January 2002).

Deadlier than the male

The history of terror took on a new image when the first female suicide bomber picked up a 10 kg bomb, packed it into a rucksack and strapped it to her back before setting off for Jerusalem.

On 27 January 2002 Waffa Idrees, a 28-year-old paramedic, ran out from an alley into Jaffa Street in West Jerusalem, a busy Jewish neighbourhood, filled with shops and restaurants ... and blew herself to pieces killing an elderly bystander and seriously injuring 100 other people.

This young woman was a volunteer first-aider with the Palestinian Red Crescent in Ramallah, a stretcher-bearer who was used to dashing into the thick of the fighting to recover the bodies of the Palestinian youth who had been injured or even killed.

Idrees is being celebrated as a heroine; she represents a new phenomenon in Israel. Until now the suicide terrorists have always been male, now it seems a **new breed** of radical, young Palestinian women are rising up ready to seek martyrdom.

She was known to be a good friend and a loving daughter. Among those who will be celebrating her death will be one

Suicide bomber holding a copy of the Koran

woman who will be singing her praises even louder than the rest. This will be her mother because in Islam it is a great honour to be the mother of a martyr for *jihad* or **holy war for Allah**.

Time to pray

In total contrast the God of Israel is doing awesome things in the hearts and minds of would be suicide bombers and terrorists – as a growing number are finding faith in Jesus.

Although numbering only a few hundred scattered believers throughout the West Bank, many recount direct revelation from God in visions and dreams.

For a Muslim, to change his faith is an anathema and according to the Koran, worthy of death. This may well be at the hands of their own family who would go to such extremes in order to rid this 'shame' from their family name. Those who have been working among these ex-Muslims report that many of them are as radical to their commitment to Jesus as they have been in their commitment to Mohammed.

God has been doing such a heart transplant in these Palestinians, the result being that His love and forgiveness is replacing the hatred, anger and bitterness they once felt towards Israel. Not only so, but as they read the Bible for themselves, some are beginning to see God's covenant with the Jewish people and are praying faithfully for the restoration and salvation of Israel.

Consequently these Palestinian ex-Muslims refuse to take part in the current Intifada. Many have been arrested by the Palestinian Authority (PA) and without trial thrown into prison on trumped up allegations, where they undergo the most horrendous torture.

An increasing number are now on the run or in hiding after receiving threats of imprisonment by the PA, often leaving large families struggling without a breadwinner to provide for them.

May the Lord keep us faithful in upholding our Palestinian brothers in prayer and practical aid, until the love of Jesus spreads like a fire throughout this troubled region.

Their faith is truly the greatest witness to the resurrection of Israel's Messiah and because of Him this people have not only had their hearts changed towards Israel and the Jewish people, but they are willing to lay down their lives, not in the cause of *Jiajd* or the Holy War for Allah, but for the **peace of Jerusalem** in the name of the God of Abraham, Isaac and Jacob – the God of Israel.

Chapter 17

A Call to Repentance

Global terror

'Made in Israel' security devices ranging from self-opening para-chutes designed for escape from burning skyscrapers, to flying platforms designed to rise up the sides of tower blocks and carry stranded terror or disaster victims to safety, are being supplied to a world threatened by global terror.

Since the 11 September attack, tens of thousands of orders have been pouring into Israel for gas masks. The fear of terrorist attacks with chemical or biological weapons has caused increasing numbers of governments and businessmen seeking Israeli expertise needed on security devices.

Terror and war have driven away tourists and foreign investors from Israel, taxes have risen and the economy has suffered. Israelis have been forced to devote much of their ingenuity and resources into protecting themselves.

The Western world is turning to Israel for safety devices to combat the invisible enemy of terrorism in their midst.

Many Israeli companies who specialise in airport security, the training of guards and who are staffed by veterans of specialised army units have been in high demand, their expertise ranging from security devices to consultancy in preparing for biological germ warfare.

Israeli security has always had a good reputation amounting to almost one-tenth of Israel's 2.5 billion dollar defence exports in the year 2000. However, since 11 September there has been a sharp increase in the demand for 'Made in Israel' security.[1]

> ' "Not by might nor by power, but by My Spirit,"
> Says the LORD of hosts.'   (Zechariah 4:6)

---

[1] Excerpts from *Jerusalem Report*, 17 December 2001.

After more than fifty years of ongoing war against terrorism it is easy to understand how a predominantly secular Israel has learned to rely on her own strength and ingenuity in her times of need.

Israel, however, is not only competing with the West in her technology but also in her debauchery. Domestic violence, alcoholism, drugs, prostitution, homosexuality and abortion are rife.

Is the God of Abraham, Isaac and Jacob, indifferent to Israel's sin?

Is the Almighty who has called Himself her husband, going to stand by and allow her to follow further down the path of adultery?

Will not the God of Israel who has declared His love for her with an everlasting love, chastise her in His mercy?

> *'You shall be called Hephzibah* [my delight is in her],
>   *and your land Beulah* [married],
> *For the* Lord *delights in you,*
> *And your land shall be married.'*   (Isaiah 61:4)

> *' "And it shall be, in that day,"*
> *Says the* Lord,
> *"That you will call Me 'My Husband,'*
> *And no longer call Me 'My Master,'* ...
> *I will betroth you to Me forever;*
> *Yes, I will betroth you to Me*
> *In righteousness and justice,*
> *In lovingkindness and mercy;*
> *I will betroth you to Me in faithfulness,*
> *And you shall know the* Lord*." '*   (Hosea 2:16, 19)

Surely the day is coming upon Israel when she will no longer find the answers in her own strength and abilities but only in the faithfulness of her God.

Then and now

For centuries the land of Israel was barren and sterile, neglected and ignored even by its conquerors. In the 1800s when the first wave of *aliyah* began to take place and the Jewish people (inspired by the vision of the Promised Land, a land flowing with milk and honey) began to irrigate and farm malaria-ridden swamps purchased from the Arabs ... the rains began to fall.

The Lord was faithful to fulfil His promises in Deuteronomy 11:14–17 to provide 'rain for the land in its season,' but He warned Israel that 'If they turned aside and served other gods and worshipped them, His anger would be aroused and He would shut up the heavens so that there would be no rain.'

Where is the rain?

God does not leave us in ignorance. There are signs occurring in Israel today. One in particular is decreased rainfall; Israel's water supply is now seriously depleted. The country is facing its deepest and most severe water crisis ever, the result of mismanagement, over-pumping and three years of drought. There is serious risk of irreversible deterioration of water quality at various resources.

Desalination plants already planned won't be ready for three years and it will be 16 months before water can be pumped in from Turkey. This, plus the fact that Israelis are not willing to conserve their water, does not present a very optimistic forecast.

In the near future, water, not oil, may be the most valuable commodity in the Middle East.

In just over a year the Tigris and Euphrates Rivers will, for the first time in history, be under the control of humanity. The downstream countries of Iran, Iraq and Syria may well observe with envy **the greener grass on the other side of the Israeli fence**, and who knows whether these Arab nations, with weapons of mass destruction ... but no water ... will attack this tiny and vulnerable nation?

Could it be that the God of Abraham, Isaac and Jacob, is waiting for His chosen Jewish people, *'the apple of His eye'*, to cry out to Him, the Only One who can protect them and save their land?

> *'If My people who are called by My name will humble themselves, and pray and seek My face, and turn from their wicked ways, then I will hear from heaven, and will forgive their sin and heal their land.'*   (2 Chronicles 7:14)

Could it be, that like the West, Israel too, has turned her back on her Creator, the Maker of heaven and earth, the God of Israel? Could it be that, she too, is flouting the God-given laws of the Bible?

'Believe in the LORD *your God, and you shall be established; believe His prophets, and you shall prosper.'*

(2 Chronicles 20:20)

God is the only answer.

'For I will pour water on him who is thirsty,
And floods on the dry ground.' (Isaiah 44:3)

The enemy waits at the door. But we know God goes with His people through the fire and delivers them **in it**.

'Behold, I have refined you, but not as silver;
I have tested you in the furnace of affliction.' (Isaiah 48:10)

Chapter 18

'Where There Is No Vision the People Perish'

(Proverbs 29:18 AV)

Hooked by the vision

God is sending His fishermen to bring back the Jewish people to the land and to fulfil His Word. Zionists with an understanding of God's purposes for Israel have obeyed the call of God to help with the final re-gathering of God's people.

All efforts to enable the Jews to make *aliyah*, which is the Hebrew word for 'ascending' or 'going up to Zion', would be of no avail if the Lord had not first planted the vision into the hearts of His own people, who have hoped and prayed throughout the centuries for the re-gathering of the exiles and the restoration of Zion.

Like fish caught on the divine hook of prophecy, God's people have been filled with a fervent desire to see a sovereign Jewish state in *eretz* Israel.

> '*Hope deferred makes the heart sick,*
> *But when the desire comes, it is a tree of life.*'

(Proverbs 13:12)

Restoration of Israel and the Church

The attitude of Christians towards Jews changed during the sixteenth and seventeenth centuries, when the Bible became available to scholars and laymen alike, after it had been translated into English, the everyday language of the people. Up until then only the intellectual elite, who could read Latin and Greek, could understand the scriptures. The Bible was the exclusive property of the Church. As the Word of God began to spread through the move of the Holy Spirit and the apostolic preaching of men like John Wesley and George Whitefield, a new awakening came to the Christian Church bringing with it fresh revelation and renewed interest in the restoration of the Jews.

At the time of the French Revolution in 1789 and Napoleon's invasion of Egypt and Palestine in 1798, interest in eschatology began to grow and evangelical Christians who had some understanding of the end times began to prophesy that England would be used by God in the restoration of Israel.

A change of climate in the English Church resulting in a growing hunger for a more spiritual reality was working together for the good, both for the Church and for the Zionist movement. After years of religious bigotry and Replacement Theology (the false belief that the Church has replaced Israel), revelation brought new light and understanding. God was not finished with the Jewish people.

The fires of evangelical revival in the eighteenth and nineteenth centuries which swept through England were not coincidental, but clear evidence of God's promise to bless those who bless Israel:

> 'I will make you a great nation;
> I will bless you
> And make your name great;
> And you shall be a blessing.
> I will bless those that bless you,
> And curse him that curses you;
> And in you all the families of the earth shall be blessed.'
>
> (Genesis 12:2–3)

Blessings and curses

> 'But the LORD plagued Pharaoh and his house with great plagues because of Sarai, Abram's wife.'   (Genesis 12:17)

The persecution of the Jews in AD 364 under the Emperor Constantine, and his anti-Semitic laws, preceded the break-up of his empire.

In 1492 300,000 Spanish Jews were expelled from Spain. Spain's fall from power also dates back to this time.

When Egypt blessed Joseph and his family, she prospered. When she enslaved the children of Israel and refused to release them she brought curses upon herself.

Britain was once the greatest empire in the world under Queen Victoria. During this time Benjamin Disraeli was Prime Minister. Disraeli, who was a Jewish Christian, played a significant role in the Jewish struggle for emancipation and was a Zionist at heart. Under his title of Lord Beaconsfield, he spoke at length in the House of Lords on behalf of the Jewish people. When he saw Jerusalem for the first time he said, 'To touch her is to touch eternity.' In the book *Disraeli* by Sarah Bradford (quoting Hansard), published by Wiedenfield and Nicolson, he said:

'The Jews are persons who acknowledge the same God as the Christian people of this realm. They acknowledge the same Divine revelations as yourselves, they are, humanly speaking, the authors of your religion. They are unquestionably those to whom you are indebted for no inconsiderable portion of your own religion and for the whole of your Divine knowledge.

Where is your Christianity, if you do not believe in their Judaism? On every sacred day, you read to the people the exploits of the Jewish heroes, the proof of Jewish devotion, the brilliant annuls of past Jewish magnificence.

Every man in the early ages of the Church by whose power, or zeal, or genius, Christian faith was propagated, is a Jew.

I, whatever the consequences – must speak what I feel, I cannot sit in this House with any misconception of my opinion on the subject. Whatever may be the consequences on the seat I hold – I cannot, for one, give a vote which is not in deference to what I believe to be the true principles of religion. Yes, it is as a Christian that I will not take upon me the awful responsibility of excluding from the legislature those who are of the religion in the bosom of which my Lord and Saviour was born.'

There have been many British Zionists who longed to see the day of the restoration of Israel. Sir Moses Montefiore, a Jewish banker and philanthropist, was Sheriff of London in 1837, when Queen Victoria came to the throne. He was the founder of modern Jerusalem and a famous windmill overlooking the old city stands as a memorial to him.

Sir Lawrence Oliphant, a member of the British Parliament, who served as a soldier, diplomat, journalist and author, and was also a scholar of the Russian language, was instrumental in aiding Jews who were able to escape the pogroms that were sweeping across Europe around 1878. He moved to Haifa with his wife, sacrificing his comfortable lifestyle in England, in order to help the Jews who began to arrive from Russia. He enabled them to start a new life in the agricultural settlements that were set up by these Jewish refugees from persecution

On 2 November 1917, Arthur J. Balfour, the British Foreign Secretary, issued what has come to be known as the Balfour Declaration:

> 'His Majesty's Government view with favour the establishment in Palestine of a national home for the Jewish people, and will use their best endeavours to facilitate the achievement of this object, it being clearly understood that nothing shall be done which may prejudice the civil and religious rights of the existing non-Jewish communities in Palestine, or the rights of political status enjoyed by Jews in any other country.'

Just over a month later Palestine was liberated from the Turks on 11 December 1917, during World War I under General Edmund Allenby, ending the 400-year rule of the Ottoman Empire. Allenby prayed that there would be no bloodshed and the next day the Turks fled. Allenby entered Jerusalem on foot without a shot being fired on the first day of Chanukah. God's timing is always perfect.

The Lord has promised to bring His people home:

> 'For I will take you from among the nations, gather you out of all countries, and bring you into your own land.'   (Ezekiel 36:24)

Many courageous men and women have willingly dedicated their lives to this cause. The list of names would fill the pages of another book and even as the author writes, many are rising to the challenge, knowing that as we, the Church, pray for the peace of Jerusalem and give ourselves to His purposes for the Jewish people and their return to the land of Israel, we will be preparing the way for the Messiah to come once again to His people … this time in answer to their call.

Fishers and hunters

> ' "*Therefore behold, the days are coming," says the* LORD, "*that it shall no more be said, 'The* LORD *lives who brought up the children of Israel from the land of Egypt,' but, 'The* LORD *lives who brought up the children of Israel from the land of the north and from all the lands where He had driven them.' For I will bring them back into the land which I gave to their fathers. Behold, I will send for many fishermen," says the* LORD, "*and they shall fish them; and afterward I will send for many hunters, and they shall hunt them from every mountain and every hill, and out of the holes of the rocks.*" '
> (Jeremiah 16:14–16)

When God parted the Red Sea, more than 2 million Jews were released from captivity as slaves in Egypt. No-one was left behind.

The last exodus will be greater by far. Not only has the Lord promised to re-gather His ancient people from the four corners of the earth, but He has also promised to join them together, bone to bone, flesh to flesh, and breathe new life into them so that they will rise up together as one mighty army of the Lord (Ezekiel 37).

This spiritual awakening, described by Paul as *'life from the dead'* (Romans 11:15), will bring about the fulfilment of Jesus' prophecy to the Jewish people of Jerusalem, before He ascended into heaven:

> '*You shall see Me no more till you say, "Blessed is He who comes in the name of the* LORD.*"* '
> (Matthew 23:39)

What a day that will be when the Jewish people are gathered together in the land of their forefathers, Abraham, Isaac and Jacob, and together in one voice they cry out to their Messiah. Then and only then, will the heavens open and Jesus will return again to the very same spot from which He ascended, the Mount of Olives in Jerusalem.

Before this apocalyptic event, certain things must happen in God's order and in accordance with His Word –

1. The Jews must return, willingly or unwillingly, to the land of Israel.
2. They will cry out to their Messiah as the revelation of who He is overwhelms them.

3. They will rise up together, **united in Messiah**, a mighty army, whose weapons are no longer carnal, but spiritual (Ephesians 6).
4. The Word of the Lord shall go forth from Zion once again.
5. The true Church and believing Israel will be one new man in Jesus, the Messiah.
6. Jerusalem will arise and shine as the glory of the Lord fills the believing Jewish people with revelation and faith in Messiah in spite of their circumstances. This will be the greatest miracle of all because the Bible has given us plenty of warnings about the forces of darkness that will unleash their evil powers against Israel in the Last Days. However, as they shine like a candle, revealing God's true light in a world of darkness, the world will witness the greatest sign and wonder of all time. There will be no more room for doubt as the God of Israel reveals His true identity to, and through His people, Israel.

Then Messiah will come again to planet Earth.

'Now if their fall is riches for the world, and their failure riches for the Gentiles, how much more their fullness!'   (Romans 11:12)

'For if their rejection be the reconciliation of the world, what will their acceptance be but life from the dead?'
(Romans 11:15 ASV)

Chapter 19

The Proof of God

Substantial evidence

The most convincing evidence of Almighty God, the God of the Bible, is most clearly seen in the preservation of the Jewish people and Israel.

What better way could the Lord choose to reveal Himself to the whole world throughout the ages of mankind than to select from all the species one human family, from this family twelve tribes, and out of these tribes a nation, Israel.

To those of you who would question the reality of God and the truth of His Word, the Bible, I would say to you, keep your eyes on Israel, consider the Jews, past, present and future. If you want to know what lies ahead for all of us, Jew and Gentile, watch the news, read the Bible, then come back to me and say 'there is no God'.

If you are truly seeking the truth of an omnipotent and all-powerful Creator who wrote history (His story) and who controls the destiny of the world, keep your eyes on Israel and consider the Jews.

To those of you who were born to evangelise the world for God, who burn with the desire to preach the gospel of Jesus Messiah, I would say to you, remember the words of Jesus to the woman at the well. Lost and in need of salvation she had searched all her life through many husbands and lovers, to find the truth of love and of God. and still her thirst could not be quenched, except in Him, from whom flows the living water that will never run dry, the source of all life, truth and love.

What did He say to her?

What were the words of Jesus that brought this woman to the end of her long and lonely quest. In five simple words Jesus explained God's purpose for all mankind when He said, *'Salvation is of the Jews'* (John 4:22).

Frederick the Great of Prussia once asked his chaplain for proof of the existence of God. 'Show me a miracle,' he said. The answer came without hesitation, 'The Jews, your Majesty.'

When Napoleon was in Egypt during the Battle of the Pyramids, he was asked by one of his marshals (an atheist) if he believed there was a God. 'Gentlemen,' Napoleon answered, and he pointed to one of his marshals, a Jew, 'there is the unmistakable argument.'

'Salvation is of the Jews' (John 4:22)

> *'...they are enemies for your sake...'* (Romans 11:28)

This is my testimony. My salvation certainly was of the Jews. Even though I was raised by Christian parents, christened and confirmed in the Anglican church, educated in a Roman Catholic convent and as a small child I trusted in Jesus, who was to me the epitome of everything that is good, wise and holy, as I grew older I began to ask questions. I could find no firm foundation for my childlike faith. The physical reality I saw all around me seemed to be a million light years away from the Jesus I knew in my heart.

> Gentle Jesus, meek and mild,
> Look upon this little child,
> Pity my simplicity
> And suffer me to come to thee.

The words of Charles Wesley's famous hymn (1707–1788) were taught me by my grandmother.

This was my prayer, the prayer I had prayed each night since I was old enough to talk, on my knees beside my bed, first with my grandmother then with my mother, until I began to pray alone and my mind started to get in the way.

To an analytical mind that hungered for the truth, the traditional Church seemed nebulous, mystical and far-removed from reality.

By my early teens I had already embarked upon an acting career, leading me even deeper into the world of fantasy and superficiality, a world inhabited by the rich and famous and more often than not, desperate and impoverished souls.

I never stopped looking for the real Jesus. Not the blue and white-robed statues or the images of Him in stained glass windows with blonde hair and golden haloes. Not even the limp body hanging on a cross that I looked at day after day in the chapel of my convent school, where as a child I would often spend time alone, weeping and wondering why such a good, gentle and loving person should have suffered and died in such a way. No-one seemed to have the answers I was looking for or needed to hear.

Then, one day, an orthodox Jewish friend gave me a book called *Jewish Sources of the Sermon on the Mount*. It was the first of many books that I was to read, all written by Jews, that would eventually lead me back to the book of all books, the Bible, which for the first time in my life, I began to read from a Jewish perspective.

I became a proselyte to Judaism. I came to believe in and worship Hashem, the God of Israel, our Father, and this brought me back to the foot of the Cross, but this time my eyes were opened to see Him in all His glory and on the night I was born again, I had a vision of Him leading a mighty army into battle. He was the Lion of the tribe of Judah, the Messiah of Israel, the King of kings, coming back to His people, not as a suffering servant but this time as a mighty warrior.

In 1967 at the time of the six-day war in Israel, I remember sitting in my apartment watching the news on TV with my Bible in my hand. Jerusalem was back in Jewish hands after nearly 2,000 years since the destruction of the Temple in 70 AD.

I was watching the soldiers weeping as they touched the Wailing Wall. I remember the tears were streaming down my face as I saw all I had been reading about in the Bible coming true before my eyes.

All this was proof to me that the Bible was the Divinely-inspired Word of God and that the God of Israel I had been reading about was alive today and acting on behalf of His chosen people, the Jews.

He hadn't forsaken them in spite of their sins, which were many, and the Bible makes no attempt to hide the sins of Israel but it also tells us that God has chosen them.

> 'For Jacob My servant's sake,
> And Israel My elect,
> I have even called you by your name.'   (Isaiah 45:4)

To me the very existence of the Jewish people and the land of Israel, with Jerusalem as its capital city, is evidence of a God who promised to return them to this land, a God who has not broken His Word is true and His faithfulness endures for ever.

This was the proof I needed to believe in this God of Israel. If He could love Israel with such an everlasting love, then He could love me too and not forsake me, because He, Hashem, is a faithful God.

I needed proof. I found it in the Jewish people. I owe them a debt because through them I found my Saviour and my salvation.

The Church needs the Jewish people

Can you imagine this world without the Jewish people and without Israel? For too long the Church has arrogantly assumed we have got it all. We don't need the Jewish people, they need us. But this is so wrong.

Paul warned us in Romans 11:18 not to boast against the branches of the true olive tree, which is Israel, for we have only been grafted in. He said *'remember that you do not support the root but the root supports you.'*

The Jewish people and Israel are the root from which we draw our sustenance, without which we would have withered and died. The Jews are the vehicle God chose to bring Messiah to planet earth and through them, and only them, Messiah will return, when they cry out *'Blessed is he who comes in the name of the Lord'* (Psalm 118:26).

Without the Jewish people and Israel, where would we be?

The enemy in our midst

The wheat and the tares are growing together (see Matthew 13:24–30 and 37–40). *'The children of the kingdom'* and *'the children of the wicked one'* (Matthew 13:38 AV) are living side by side, many are also professing to be doing God's work, so much so that it is difficult to know who is who in the world and even in the church.

The devil has planted the enemy in our midst, and the Lord warned us this evil will be with us until the end of the world, and it is only by holding fast to the Word of God that we will not be deceived.

In Britain today Muslim clerics are allowed to preach openly on *jihad*. *The Guardian*, 14 February 2001, described the UK as 'a *revolving door*' to radical Islam and open to terrorist activity. Documents compiled in Milan, Hamburg, Madrid and Paris indicated that most of the terrorist attacks planned in the last four years had links to Britain. The main European centres for spiritual indoctrination and the training of potential Islamic suicide terrorists are in London and Leicester.

According to Melanie Phillips in her article 'Christians who hate the Jews' published in *The Spectator*, 16 February 2002,

> 'The ancient hatred of Jews rooted deep in Christian theology is on widespread display once again – having been revived by the Middle East conflict.'

Palestinian politics and Christian theology have become inextricably intertwined.

The doctrine 'Replacement Theology' which teaches that the Christians have '**replaced**' the Jews in God's favour, and **all** God's promises to the Jewish people **including the land of Israel** – have been inherited by the church, has re-emerged under the new heading of 'Palestinian–Christian Revisionism.'

This ancient hatred of the Jews, which was used by Hitler to fan the flames of the Holocaust, is very much alive and still with us today in many of the churches in England including the Anglican and Roman Catholic denominations.

Could this be the **new face** of anti-Semitism preparing the way for the anti-Christ Jesus warned us about in Daniel 9:27, Matthew 24:15 and Mark 13:14 – as depicted in the 'Jesus look-alike', wearing the swastika on his robes, illustrated on page 11 of this book?

What must we do?

So what does this mean to you and me? The scars inflicted by hatred of the Jewish people still remain.

Once Israel represented a safe haven to Jews, the one place in the world where they could be free from anti-Semitism. Now terrifying doubts are creeping into the heart of every Israeli. With five million Jews gathered together in one tiny strip of land, Israel is centre stage, a prime target for attack.

> 'Israel is the most dangerous place for Jews, it doesn't stop anti-Semitism, on the contrary, it generates it.'
>   (Effre Eitam, *Jerusalem Report*, 17 December 2001)

The scene is being set for the isolation of the tiny nation of Israel and the redemption of her God.

When she is all alone in a world which doesn't care if she lives or dies, who will she turn to? She is being prepared for the coming of her Messiah. What must we do?

I believe we must become like Esther, in a time when her people were under threat of extermination, as they are today:

> *'The LORD will have war with Amalek from generation to generation.'*
> (Exodus 17:16)

Whether the enemy is coming in the name of Haman, Hitler, Arafat, Osama Bin Laden or Saddam Hussein, the nature of the beast is unchanged and his intention is always to eliminate the Jewish people and Israel off the face of the earth.

Do not be silent

Mordecai's words to Esther were hard and without compromise. She was left with a choice that only she could make.

> *'Do not flatter yourself that you shall escape in the king's palace any more than all the other Jews. For if you keep silent at this time, relief and deliverance shall arise for the Jews from elsewhere, but you and your father's house will perish. And who knows but that you have come to the kingdom for such a time as this and for this very occasion?'*
> (Esther 4:13–14 AMP)

> *'And the Jews ... took it upon themselves and their descendants, **and all who joined them**, ... that these days should be remembered [imprinted on their minds] and kept throughout every generation.'*
> (Esther 9:27–28 AMP)

This warning echoes down the centuries to God's people today. If we keep silent at this time *'relief and deliverance shall arise for the Jews from elsewhere'* but what will the consequences be for the Church of the living God? Could it be that we – you and I – have come to the kingdom for such a time as this?

Esther had the courage to make a difference. What did Esther do? First she made a decision **to go all the way** for her Jewish brothers and sisters saying, *'If I perish, I perish.'* (Esther 4:16). Secondly she fasted and prayed. Thirdly she took action, she did something.

'We are to pray as if it all depended upon God and act as if it all depended upon us.'   (Charles Spurgeon)

Count the cost

We all know the story Jesus told of the sheep and the goats, the righteous and unrighteous nations. Jesus said to the righteous nations,

> *'I was hungry and you gave Me food; I was thirsty and you gave Me drink; I was a stranger and you took Me in; I was naked and you clothed Me; I was sick and you visited Me; I was in prison and you came to Me.'*   (Matthew 25:35–36)

> *'Assuredly, I say to you, inasmuch as you did do it to one of the least of these My brethren, you did it to Me.'*   (Matthew 25:40)

How much will it cost us to love those who were made enemies for our sake? Are we willing to pay the price?

History reveals to us that we have all been guilty of turning our backs on the Jewish people in their time of need. Can we afford to make the same mistakes again?

Jesus also said to the unrighteous nations,

> *'For I was hungry and you gave Me no food; I was thirsty and you gave Me no drink; I was a stranger and you did not take Me in, naked and you did not clothe Me, sick and in prison and you did not visit Me.'*   (Matthew 25:42–43)

> *'Inasmuch as you did not do it to one of the least of these, you did not do it to Me.'*   (Matthew 25:45)

Revival fire

Some time ago while watching the 'Discovery Channel' on TV, a documentary on Volcanic Eruptions, I was inspired to write a poem. That night I had a dream and the Lord woke me in the wee small hours of the morning, as He always does when He wants my **full attention.** He showed me the meaning of my dream. I wrote the words down as follows:

A dark red crack in the earth's crust
Hot magma bursting through the dust
Volcanic mountains spewing forth
Molten rock from burning cores.

I had a dream, the nations shaking
Cities crumbling the whole earth quaking
I heard the voices scream and wail
'Is this the beginning of travail?'

I asked the meaning of my dreams
God said, 'It's not the way it seems...
You see the dead and hear their cry...
But what I burn I purify.

Each fiery mountain that erupts
Enriches soil that man corrupts.
Vessels of clay – filled to the measure
Refined by fire, bring forth my treasure.

Nation rises against nation
But out of chaos comes Creation
And every city that is shaken
Will cause my people to awaken.

For in my wrath I come in power
To warn men of their final hour
Be still my child and do not fear
Travail begins – the end is near.

The pangs of birth will come and go
As from the depth new life will flow
The writhing womb of planet earth
Through travail, will bring forth new birth.

'He who has an ear, let him hear what the Spirit says to the churches.' (Revelation 2:11)

'For we must consider that we shall be as a City on a Hill. The eyes of all peoples are upon us. So that if we should deal falsely with our God in this work we have undertaken, and so cause Him to withdraw His present help from us, we shall be made a story and a byword throughout the world.'
(John Winthrop, 1588–1649.
Written on board the *Arbella* in 1630 as
the Pilgrim Fathers approached America.)

'Indeed I tremble for my country, when I reflect that God is Just.' (Thomas Jefferson, 1743–1826)

'England, Awake! Awake! Awake!
Jerusalem, thy sister calls.
Wilt thou sleep the sleep of death
And close her from thy ancient walls?'

(William Blake, 1757–1827)

Each one's work will become manifest;
for the Day will declare it, because it will be revealed by fire;
and the fire will test each one's work, of what sort it is.'
(1 Corinthians 3:13)

A Vision for Israel

The Joseph Storehouse Trust Limited is a humanitarian aid ministry that helps Jew and Arab alike in the land of Israel.

As you have read in this book the needs are great.

In 1996 after the bus bombings in Jerusalem in which their daughter lost four of their friends, Barry and Batya Segal began to visit the families of the terrorist victims and saw the shattered lives and their need for help, both practical and spiritual.

Out of this tragedy Vision for Israel began as a charity to help the people in the land of Israel.

The vision grew and in 1998 the first Joseph Storehouse was opened in Jerusalem to store and distribute food, clothing and much-needed medical equipment and humanitarian aid to help families in need.

Help began to flow in from Bible believers from all over the world and a second Joseph Storehouse was opened in Savannah, Georgia, USA.

This was followed by a third Storehouse in Storrington, West Sussex, UK, in January 2001.

Many people gathered together to join in the dedication with speakers including Reverend Canon Andrew White, the Canon of Coventry Cathedral, and the Marquis of Reading.

Today the Joseph Storehouse Trust is providing *'love in action'* for all those caught up in the unstable consequences of living in a region torn apart by hatred and where peace has become elusive.

Your assistance can be given in several ways:

1. By volunteering at the Joseph Storehouse to sort and pack aid ready for shipment.
2. By donating financially.
3. By the giving of practical aid, such as medical equipment, clothing, non-perishable foods.

You may feel you would like to help in some way. For further information please contact the Joseph Storehouse:

Telephone: (0)1903 744419
Fax: (0)1903 744415
Email: info@visionforisrael.com

or look on their website:

www.visionforisrael.com

Suggested Reading

Church, J.R., *Guardians of the Grail – And the Men Who Plan to Rule the World*. Prophecy Publications: PO Box 7000, Oklahoma City, OK 73153

Cohn, Norman, *Warrant for Genocide*. Serif: 47 Straham Road, London E3 5DA

Larsson, Goran, *Fact or Fraud? – The Protocols of the Elders of Zion*. Jerusalem Centre for Biblical Studies and Research: Israel, PO Box 8017, Jerusalem 91080

Mordecai, Victor, *Is Fanatic Islam a Global Threat?*. PO Box 18209, Jerusalem 91181

Wistrich, Robert S., *Anti-semitism – The Longest Hatred*. Thames Metheun: Michelin House, 81 Fulham Road, London SW3 6RB, in Association with Thames TV International Ltd